Autistic Spectrum
in the Early Years

A Guide for Practitioners

by
Dr Rita Jordan

A QEd Publication

Published in 2002

ISBN 1 898873 29 1

British Library Cataloguing
A catalogue record for this book is available from the British Library.

Published by QEd, The ROM Building, Eastern Avenue, Lichfield, Staffs. WS13 6RN
Web site: www.qed.uk.com
Email: orders@qed.uk.com

Printed in the United Kingdom by Stowes (Stoke-on-Trent).

Contents

Chapter One

Introduction

About this book

Autistic Spectrum Disorders (ASDs) are complex and it will not help to pretend otherwise. Nevertheless, although the numbers of children with these conditions seem to be increasing (especially in the early years), not all practitioners need to be 'experts'. What you do need is practical understanding so that you can help these children begin to learn and develop and so that problems are not exacerbated, with the child developing secondary problems or being kept out of the very learning opportunities s/he needs so much.

As a practitioner, you also need to know when and where to ask for additional help from local people with greater expertise and how to work with parents to develop mutual trust and to share knowledge and resources. Parents are usually the first to know that something is wrong, even if they do not know exactly what it is, and they can be a valuable source of information from parent support groups, the Internet and conference attendance. However, the amount of information is itself a problem (especially when some of it may be misleading) so parents too may need support in filtering the information and making informed judgements about what to use and how to apply it.

In this short book, therefore, the main areas that will cause concern are addressed, always with a practical focus on what needs to be done and the principles to guide practice. Short examples are given to illustrate points and bring them to life. In such a short book, with so much to cover, there is no time to give general special educational needs (SEN) advice on individual educational plans (IEPs), preparing information for others, observing behaviour and following the *SEN Code of Practice* (DfES, 2001), but this is one of a series and others will have all this information applied to other SEN; these guides are listed among the resources.

This book, then, is aimed at all those working with children in the early years in whatever setting, because children with ASDs (with and without diagnoses) are to be found in all such settings. It is written from a UK perspective, but most of its contents will apply across cultures and countries. It also applies across professional disciplines and to those who do not have professional qualifications but are working in early years settings. Although it is aimed at staff, it will also have something for parents of young children with an ASD (the word 'parent' is used as the generic term for those who are the primary carers). It is short enough to be read as a whole, to gain an overview, but it also contains enough practical guidance to be used afterwards as a reference guide for aspects of the curriculum or to deal with certain problems. It should not, however, be read and applied in any order since later sections depend on the understanding that comes from the initial ones.

About Autistic Spectrum Disorders (ASDs)

Many people will have heard of 'autism', and 'Asperger's syndrome' is also becoming better known, but people are often confused about how they relate to one another and about what is covered by the term 'Autistic Spectrum Disorders'. ASD is a broad term, introduced by Lorna Wing (1996). It is not a specific diagnosis, but covers a range of conditions that share what has come to be called the 'triad of impairments' and are distinguishable from other developmental disorders on that basis. The triad is confusingly defined slightly differently by different authors but the most currently accepted version is that there are developmental difficulties in:

- understanding social and emotional information and relating to others;

- understanding and using all aspects of communication, regardless of speech development;

- monitoring, controlling and being flexible in both thinking and behaviour.

It should be noted that these are developmental areas, not specific behaviours and thus there are no behaviours that are of themselves 'autistic' or peculiar to individuals with an ASD. That is why it makes little sense to speak of 'autistic features' or 'traits' and especially not 'autistic tendencies'. The latter is very unhelpful, giving the worrying idea that someone might suddenly 'become' autistic, without giving any idea of how they should be treated. Disturbances in all three aspects of development should be there in an ASD and it is the interaction between these areas of development that leads to the characteristically complex patterns of behaviour seen in ASDs.

By focusing only on a single aspect of the triad, it is not clear if the difficulties are due to an ASD or to an entirely different cause and, as later sections will show, this information matters. We interpret behaviour differently if we suspect it arises through an ASD and so treatment and approach will also need to be different. For example, a severely abused and traumatised child will show many of the behavioural features associated with autism, but s/he will 'recover' if given sustained tender loving care and support. The problem with many cases of child abuse is that they do not get this sustained treatment, but go from one unsatisfactory situation to another, so then there is no recovery. However, in ASDs, there has almost certainly been no abuse or trauma and it is the parents' attempts at tender loving care that the child has been unable to understand or deal with. Just giving them more of the same is not going to help, and is likely instead to send them further into retreat or rage. We need to approach them first on their terms and gradually teach the adjustments that will enable them to accept our well-meant approaches.

Questions about ASDs

Can I do harm if I treat a child as if they had an ASD when it later turns out they have not?

The short answer to this is 'no'. Of course there may be harmful effects from mislabelling a child but, if the child is having difficulties with the three areas identified as the triad, it is likely in any case that they have special needs that are closely related to those arising from an ASD. Treating them 'as if' they had an ASD is likely to be the best option in that nothing you will do (as long as the possibility that it is not an ASD is remembered) will harm the child or do anything other than make it easier for the child to learn and adapt to his/her environment. If it is not an ASD, this will usually quickly become apparent.

Does it matter whether a child has Asperger's syndrome, autism or some other label within ASDs?

It matters whether a child has good structural language skills and no additional learning difficulties so a diagnosis of Asperger's syndrome will usually signify that is the case and enable you to plan accordingly. However, the category is used differently by different diagnosticians and there is little evidence that 'Asperger's syndrome' differs from what is called 'high functioning autism'. It does matter if a child has 'Childhood disintegrative disorder' because, as the name implies, there is liable to be significant biologically based deterioration after the age of three and thus there is a need for particular kinds of support for the child and the family. The same applies to Rett's syndrome, where again there is a particular pattern of physical deterioration that needs to be accommodated. Yet in general, there are greater individual differences within a category such as 'autism' than there are between autism, Asperger's syndrome or atypical autism. The best advice, then, is to pay attention to the fact that the child has an ASD (that enables a different interpretation of the behaviour) but then to go to the level of the individual needs and strengths.

Can inadequate parenting lead to autism?

There is absolutely no evidence that this is the case although, as seen above, it may be that the results of child abuse may temporarily be confused with autism. We know that ASDs are largely genetic disorders although early treatment can have important effects on later development.

If a child has significant learning difficulties, does it matter if they also have an ASD?

It does matter, perhaps even more than in the more able, where the person may be able to live independently, without the need to relate to others to any significant degree. People with autism and additional learning difficulties will always need additional support and so it is very important for their future quality of life that they learn to tolerate others and co-operate with them.

Are all children with ASDs potential 'Rainmen'?

Sadly, not all children with ASDs have special talents and abilities, and certainly not at any extraordinary level. However, 'savant' skills, as they are called, are much more common in people with ASDs than in any other group, and current research is trying to find out why this is. Many individuals with an ASD, for example, will have perfect pitch, be able to memorise large chunks of material word for word or can reproduce what they have seen (in paintings) or heard (in music or speech) exactly, after one exposure. Such talents can be used and developed to the point where they provide a living for the adult with the ASD (see Stephen Wiltshire's drawings, for example) but it is more common for them to be 'dead-end' skills which do not really reflect the child's capacity to learn and acquire useful knowledge and skills.

Can autism be caused by MMR vaccination?

No one claims that MMR is the cause of most cases of ASDs, since autism pre-dates MMR and most people who get MMR do not develop ASDs. The evidence supports the view that MMR is safe for the majority of infants and will not lead to ASDs; indeed most children will be safer having an MMR than risking getting measles or mumps with their known side effects. Yet ASDs are a very heterogeneous group and it is possible that there is a group with very specific vulnerabilities who are at risk of ASDs after MMR vaccination. General epidemiological data would not pick up such a group so this is an area worthy of research in spite of the fact that most children will be unaffected.

Chapter Two

Diagnoses, special needs and labelling

Why a diagnosis matters

Diagnosis of the syndromes that constitute ASDs is a medical matter, since these categories are medical ones, yet good practice in diagnosis is that it should be a multidisciplinary process, involving early years practitioners, wherever appropriate. Diagnosis is based on a medical categorical model, but in reality each of the three developmental areas affected in ASDs represent dimensions along which people may vary from 'normal' through to 'abnormal', depending on the degree to which the person's adaptive functioning is affected. It is only when a person is at an abnormal level along each of the three dimensions of the triad that they can be considered as having an ASD. For example, we all become less flexible when we are anxious but this is only a concern when we are anxious most of the time and it only indicates an ASD when there are also problems understanding communication (especially facial expressions and gestures) and relating to others (especially other children) as well.

Early diagnosis is important in ASDs, but only if it results in intervention and support for the family. Diagnosis, therefore, should be followed by assessment of the child's needs and strengths, since these are the important factors in determining special educational needs. There is nothing worse than to be told that your child has a complex and severe developmental disorder and then for nothing to be done about it for another six months or so. It is vital that parents are given support in managing their child as soon as concerns are evident and that services for the child and family do not wait for a formal diagnosis. As was pointed out in Chapter One, the least damaging assumption is that the child has an ASD and it is worth proceeding on that basis until it is demonstrated otherwise, while explaining to parents that we are dealing with the behaviour at present while waiting to have a diagnosis confirmed.

The route to diagnosis can come from any early years practitioner or health professional or the parents concerned. In educational contexts the *SEN Code of Practice* (DfES, 2001) will give guidance on staged responses to meeting a child's special educational needs, but diagnosis is subtly different. It is only one factor in determining a child's needs, but it is a very important factor in ASDs because it transforms the meaning of the behaviour seen and thus the nature of the special needs that arise.

For example, a young child may appear to be behaving very aggressively in the playgroup towards the other children, hitting them and running off for no apparent reason, laughing when they cry, and biting, or poking their eyes when they try to be friendly and get close to him. Without the context of a diagnosis, practitioners may well discuss the situation with the parents to get a picture of the child at home, only to find there is no problem with aggression at home (he is an only child), but parents are concerned that he is very 'wilful' and independent, climbing on tables and cupboards to get what he wants, and that he sleeps very little. Seeing how exhausted the parents are, it might be concluded that the child has simply got 'out of hand' and a simple behavioural approach might be introduced to try to bring his behaviour under control. Some aspects of a behavioural approach can be effective in ASDs, but only if the autism is taken into account in understanding what is going on. If this child has an ASD, he is not going to be responsive to social disapproval, and a sharp 'NO!' every time he bites, pokes or hits will become predictable and therefore function like a reward for him, increasing this difficult behaviour. Distraction would be good, but if he is led away from the situation under the control of an adult, this will be aversive for him and he is liable to react with genuine aggression, making the situation much worse.

Staff may, however, decide to act 'as if' he has an ASD, talking it over with parents and either seeking further assessment towards diagnosis at the same time, or waiting to see if treating the child in this way will be effective, before taking further steps. That will mean they recognise that the original apparent 'aggression' stems from a lack of understanding and skill; the child is trying to get the other children to play the one game he understands and enjoys – chase. He has learnt behaviourally that hitting others and running off leads to being chased, first by the children and then by the teachers, anxious to remonstrate. Although he enjoys chase, he does not enjoy, and is terrified by, close physical contact with others, especially when they have initiated it without warning and hence his lashing out by biting and poking the offending 'objects'. Laughing at another's distress comes simply from not understanding what it is and just reacting to the peculiar noise and distortion of the face.

The steps to take then become clearer. First, he will need to be taught other ways of getting children to play chase with him and they will have to be taught what his behaviour 'means' and how they can help him (and avoid being attacked). Then he will need a programme to 'get used to' others so that he can begin to tolerate being in groups, being approached by others and having others look at him. It will be a bit much at this stage to expect him to tolerate touch, so the others will need to be taught what he can and cannot manage and how to warn him when they are coming near and not to rush up to him. This is hard for other children but, once they realise that the child has a problem and that they can help, it is amazing how thoughtful and resourceful even young children can be. Gradually we can build up the child's repertoire of interactive skills with both staff and other children (playing musical games can help as will be seen in later chapters) and increase his physical activity so we can help regularise his sleep pattern. Parents can also begin to join support groups or at least be aware of the literature, in particular, in this case, resources on dealing with sleep problems. A much more positive atmosphere then surrounds the child, who will still occasionally resort to his former ways of establishing control, but should be becoming more socially skilful and less terrified and so also be enjoying a far more positive experience.

Cumine et al. (2000) have a good guide for early years practitioners on what to look for that would lead to the suspicion of an ASD in a pre-school child. Children are very individual in their development, especially at this stage, and we do not want to see every shy or self-contained child as a child with an ASD. There are also many reasons other than an ASD why a child may become aggressive or act wildly. There needs to be a balance struck between being aware of the possibility, and seeing autism in every act of naughtiness!

Special needs arising from an ASD

Special needs are very individual, deriving from a combination of particular strengths and weaknesses in a particular context. Nevertheless, there are particular needs that derive directly from the ASD and so are likely to be shared, at least to some degree, by all those who have an ASD. As might be expected, these fall into the areas of development identified as the 'triad of impairments' that define ASDs.

Needs arising from difficulties in social and emotional understanding

The emphasis here is on understanding, because it is not simply a matter of not having social skills. There are lots of reasons why a child may fail to develop (or be delayed in developing) social skills, but in ASDs the failure or extreme delay stems from a biologically based failure to recognise social and emotional signals so the situation is far more complex. We cannot simply teach the child the missing skills (although we may have to try to do this for some key skills, as a behaviour management strategy) because the child is not equipped to learn them in the normal way.

The feature of social skills is that they are finely attuned to the social context. The child learns quickly that it is fine to rush up and hug mummy or daddy (especially when you are little) but that you should not do this to strangers, without the approval of a key adult such as a parent. But, if we try to teach children with ASDs to tolerate being hugged by their parents (and not to regard it as an assault, as many of them do, to the extreme hurt of their parents) they are likely not to make this distinction. Conversely, they may over-discriminate and only tolerate hugging from mummy when she is wearing the perfume and the clothes she had on, on the first day. This is where the interaction between the areas of the triad comes in. There is a social difficulty, which means the behaviour is not regulated by the normal social and emotional cues, and then there is a problem in learning what aspects of context are relevant and what are not, in order to apply the learnt behaviour appropriately.

14

On a more positive front, early years practitioners are in a good position to introduce some of the early social interaction experiences that the child will have missed and so help him/her to both tolerate these interactions and, through experience, to understand social experiences better and to become more aware of social and emotional cues. The child needs to learn to get pleasure from one-to-one interaction with others, to share attention, to learn the significance of eye-gaze (both mutual, and directed at objects), to regulate levels of arousal, to take turns, to become aware of the social effects of their own actions, and to learn to time interactions. These are all areas normally learnt long before a child enters a nursery or pre-school environment and they are areas of development that do not normally have to be taught in this deliberate and explicit way. However, the normal skills of interacting with a baby will serve well as a teaching technique as long as we remember to slow them down, give long and exaggerated pauses for the child's response and pick up and use whatever it is that the child can offer to the exchange at first – no matter how bizarre. Remember that mothers take their babies' 'burps' and count them as intentional communication when they are teaching the baby to develop interactive meaning. It will feel odd doing this with a much older infant or child, and one who may be well developed in other ways (physically, perhaps with good speech), but it is essential for later social interactive development. Using music can help us slow down, repeat and exaggerate in a way that is necessary but that may make us self-conscious without the aid of that music.

Emotional understanding comes from understanding ourselves first and only later understanding others. Thus, it is not a matter of sitting a child down in front of 'happy' and 'sad' faces and teaching the child to discriminate, since this is just as likely to be misleading, even if it is successful. What is far more important is that parents and staff are on the lookout for real emotions where they are sure of the emotion the child is experiencing. That is when it is important to draw the child's attention to their own emotion, demonstrate some of its manifestations (including showing the child his/her own face in a mirror) and labelling that emotion for them. Then one can move on to showing what has led up to it and, if you want to develop some behavioural control, what it is you want them to do to express that emotion other than what it is they have done. Regular drawing attention to real emotional experiences will begin to help them understand what they are. Only then will it make sense to look for signs of those emotions in others, and still later in schematised 'happy' and 'sad' faces.

Needs arising from difficulties with communication

ASDs are the only conditions in which language and communication take separate developmental paths. In all other cases, communication precedes language so that the child who is not speaking may nevertheless understand a lot of what is said and can normally understand and use a lot of communicative gestures such as pointing, looking, and changing facial expressions and body postures. However, although some children with an ASD may not be speaking, that is an additional problem. There will be others who apparently have good speech and yet do not understand speech at the level (and certainly not the speed) at which they themselves speak, do not understand any of the social nuances or non-literal meaning of the words used, and have no understanding of any of the non-verbal aspects of communication. Our natural reaction to a child who is not speaking is to slow down and speak in shorter sentences. But we have no natural reaction to meet the case of ASDs and we are liable, without a conscious effort, to interpret their lack of understanding instead as wilful, and to see the problem as a behavioural one.

First, then, the child has a need to be in an environment where people understand the true nature of his/her communication difficulties and adjust their own speech to take account of the processing problems. In addition, they will need specific teaching in gaining and switching attention in real-life contexts, in sharing attention, in using pointing both to request and to point out aspects of the environment, in how to interpret non-literal language, communicative gestures, tone of voice, intonation patterns and facial expressions. Some of this will need to be done in specific and explicit teaching sessions, but it will also need to be reinforced through drawing attention to it in daily activities. Secondly, the child will need to be taught to use a form of communication. If the child is speaking, this is more straightforward, although staff may need the support of a speech and language therapist to show them how to develop the speech towards a wider use of communicative functions other than 'request' or 'protest' – the two functions after which the child with an ASD often gets 'stuck'. If the child has no speech then some pictorial form of communication (as in TEACCH, PECS or Makaton – see Chapter Six) is essential as early as possible and some aspects of this will be useful, even for the child who has speech. A child who cannot understand speech may be able to understand sung instructions and again the use of singing, which is often natural when dealing with a younger child, may be a helpful accompaniment to everyday activities as a form of commentary.

Needs arising from difficulties with flexibility of thinking and behaviour
The child's prime need is to be understood and for others to recognise the genuine, biologically based, difficulties in planning, monitoring and thus controlling behaviour. They have problems with impulse control and so staff need to be aware that they will need to be trained in an alternative action, and directed to do that, rather than just being expected to 'stop' doing something. They also need training in planning their actions, in making choices, in recognising the consequences of their actions (and at what point in the process they have a choice), in developing other ways to play with materials, in tolerating interference in set routines, in having visual charts to give meaning and order to events, instead of relying on these inflexible patterns, and in developing good habits for work and play. In all this, there must be respect for their fear of being controlled by others and so they need to have rules to guide them (and be taught to adhere to the rules rather than to someone's command) and to manage their own panic when they have a phobic reaction and need help to get away from the phobic object.

It can be seen that in order to increase the child's flexibility, the environment itself must be flexible enough to accommodate the child's developing needs. At the beginning the child may need a very distraction-free environment that clearly indicates where to direct attention. The child may need to be sat where others are not passing (a situation that often arouses strong fear) and needs to know what to do in order to 'escape' when things get too difficult. S/he will need careful observation so that you can identify the key indicators of stress in this particular child and learn thus to pre-empt trouble by assisting that escape. Later, the child can be taught to notice these same indicators and to 'self-remove'. The priority is to adjust the environment as much as is needed initially to enable the child to relax and begin to learn. Once that process has begun, the child can be taught gradually to tolerate more stimulation and to communicate her/his needs more directly. Helping the child learn to play in ways that others play (while still respecting his/her need to have time to play in his/her own way) will increase the opportunities for that child to mix with others and develop social skills and appropriate behaviour.

Additional special needs

There is nothing in ASDs that protects the child from developing or having other special needs, either arising from an accompanying disorder such as a language impairment, sensory or physical problems, general learning difficulties or attention deficit hyperactivity disorder (ADHD), or as a secondary problem to those arising from the ASD. Where there is an additional special need, the child must have this taken into account, alongside those arising directly from the ASD. It is not a question of which is more important as both are important and will have an interactive effect. Sometimes the results are more or less subsumed into those of the ASD, for example the difficulties of intending, monitoring, and controlling actions that are a feature of both ASDs and ADHD. Sometimes they are more or less additive, as when a child with an ASD also has a hearing or a physical problem. Sometimes the interaction is particularly severe, when the needs from one block or adversely affect the prime compensatory teaching strategies of the other. Thus a child who has an ASD and also a visual loss is peculiarly disadvantaged in that the main teaching approach used in ASDs is a visual one. It is possible to develop a non-visual structured approach to teaching, but there is nothing available as a 'package' and staff and parents have to work very hard to try to find ways in which to tackle the child's difficulties.

Issues of labelling

There are still some areas, especially in early years education, where the official policy is 'not to label children'. As we have seen, it is important not to wait upon a diagnostic label before taking action, but that is not the same as saying that we should not label or that a diagnosis has no effect on special needs identification. Of course no one wants to give a child a wrong 'label' and the risk of wrong diagnosis (or of not being sure) increases the earlier the diagnosis is made in ASDs. With a trend for earlier diagnosis, there will be increasing situations where local teams will not be sure and will need to 'wait and see', taking more observations or getting more reports, before reaching a final decision. There will also be more difficult cases where there may be a need for referral on to tertiary diagnostic services in regional or even national centres. As long as everyone is honest, and the child and family are getting appropriate support, this kind of 'wait and see' is prudent. However, it is not prudent, and is not in the child's or family's best interests, to refuse a diagnostic label on ideological grounds.

The idea that if we deny a label we are somehow protecting the child from the harmful effects of labelling is in any case mistaken. Children attract labels naturally, because it is part of the normal categorisation that characterises human thinking; the issue then is whether we have labels that help to make sense for staff and family, and give access to the necessary supports, or whether we abrogate responsibility and let the child attract labels such as 'naughty', 'rude', 'stupid', 'aggressive', 'stubborn', 'lazy', 'thick' and so on. It does not take much imagination to see which labels are more harmful to attitudes, to gaining help, and to the child's own self-esteem. It is inevitable that, as 'autism' has become better known, it too is coming to be used as a term of playground abuse. That, however, is an issue of educating others, not of denying its usefulness as part of recognising a child's needs. It is attitudes to difference that need to be addressed, not the labels that help us make sense of that difference.

Chapter Three

Understanding Autistic Spectrum Disorders

What's in a name?

As we have seen, many of the subcategories within the autistic spectrum do not make much difference when it comes to working out special needs and deciding on treatment. However, many parents will attach importance to the exact category and there may well be social reasons for preferring one category over another. Here, then, is a very brief guide to some of the common categories within the spectrum, remembering that all of the categories in the spectrum will share the triad of impairments – social, communication and flexibility.

- *Autism (also 'infantile autism', 'classic autism', 'Kanner's autism')*
  This is the 'core' disorder but is now not considered to be numerically the greatest in the spectrum. Three-quarters of those with autism will have some degree of additional learning difficulty and there are frequently associated language problems. Children often start as classically withdrawn in the early years, although they may later develop more social interests. Play is likely to be stereotyped and there is great dependence on rituals. The ratio of males to females is around 4:1.

- *Asperger's syndrome (also 'Asperger syndrome/disorder')*
  Diagnostic criteria vary but there should be no additional learning difficulties (some having very high levels of general cognitive ability) and no problems in acquiring the structural aspects of speech (i.e. speaking in sentences). Some diagnosticians now use this category in preference to 'high functioning autism', regardless of whether there has been any language delay. It is the fastest growing category in ASDs, accounting for much of the increase in numbers. Rather than stereotyped play, this group is more characterised by obsessional interests but this may not be so apparent in the early years. There is

often later diagnosis of this group because of the language skills and because the real problems are not so apparent until the child begins to mix with peers. However, it should not be assumed that this is 'mild' autism (in spite of what is often written) since the autism itself may in fact be very severe. The ratio of males to females is around 14:1.

- *High functioning autism (also 'able autism')*
  This is indistinguishable from Asperger's syndrome except that there may have been initial language delay. Some have claimed this group to be less focused on people than the Asperger's group, but there is evidence of both groups having some individuals who are person-focused and some who are not. As with Asperger's syndrome, the autism itself may be mild or severe, but there are no additional general learning difficulties. Male/female ratios are not certain but are likely to be similar to the Asperger's group.

- *Pervasive developmental disorder*
  This is a term used mainly in America and is roughly equivalent to the term Autistic Spectrum Disorder.

- *Rett's syndrome*
  This mainly affects girls and is a degenerative disorder which looks most like autism in the early years and then shows improvement in sociability (although there is still often a marked lack of social understanding and indiscriminate social behaviour) just as there is marked physical deterioration. There is progressive loss of hand function, with a characteristic wringing of the hands, and there is often associated scoliosis of the spine. There are accompanying severe learning difficulties.

- *Childhood disintegrative disorder (also Heller's syndrome)*
  Here there is a marked overall deterioration after the age of two (commonly at three) with a loss of skills far in excess of the loss of the early stages of language, which is frequently seen in autism. Progressive deterioration continues and there is no recovery, although education and treatment can help arrest or slow deterioration and provide a better current quality of life. It is very rare.

- *Atypical autism (pervasive developmental disorder not otherwise specified)*
  This is a rag-bag category for those cases that appear like autism, but do not quite reach diagnostic criteria for autistic conditions. It is much less used now that Asperger's syndrome is more recognised, and many have argued that awareness of more subtle symptoms would enable these cases to be assigned to other categories. It is meant to cover cases where only two of the three areas of the triad are affected. However, this negates the whole specificity of ASDs and in my experience it is often used when the person diagnosing has failed to distinguish communication from language or has taken the third area of the triad as referring to a lack of imagination, rather than a lack of flexibility.

ASDs as developmental disorders

ASDs are developmental disorders, and this has a number of implications:

ASDs change over time

In the first case, like all developmental disorders, there will be changes in the way that the autism manifests itself over time just because of this development, apart from changes that may be brought about by treatment and education. The child may start off as timid and withdrawn, shut off from all contact, but may gradually become more responsive until eventually the child is actively seeking contact, albeit on his/her own terms.

ASDs are transactional disorders

A transactional disorder is one where the disorder both affects and is affected by others; this is very much the case in ASDs. If we take the first two areas of the triad, for example, we can see clearly that the nature of the disorder changes, depending on whose perspective we take. After all, if we are saying that these children have problems in socially interacting with us, then does that not mean we have equal difficulty in socially interacting with them? If we say that the child has a difficulty in communicating with us, are we not equally saying that we have a difficulty communicating with the child? Even when it comes to flexibility, we have to acknowledge that the child's flexibility increases to the extent that we display flexibility in adjusting to the child, so that the levels of flexibility depend on one another. When we are dealing with young children, especially, we must assume that we are the ones with the greatest capacity to understand and make the necessary adjustments to enable the child to manage the interactions better. We will also need to teach the child how to adapt and make changes, but to begin with we will be making the first moves to engage and involve the child in his/her learning.

The levels of understanding
As a developmental disorder, ASDs can be viewed at different levels.

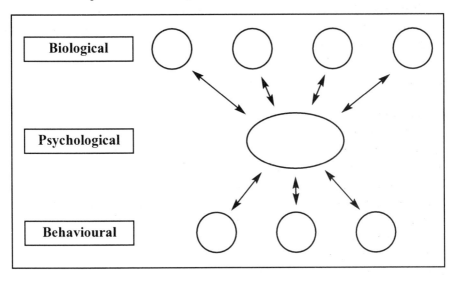

I have drawn four circles at the biological level, although in reality there may be more, and the number and kind of biological causes may differ from one case to another. We know there is a strong genetic link that involves more than one gene and that there are other biological factors involved. Apart from the worry this causes to parents over other offspring and wondering whether diets or other biological treatments might help, the actual biological cause has little impact on the day-to-day work of the practitioner.

Skipping to the behavioural level, there are three circles, representing the triad of impairments through which ASDs are recognised. Behaviour is important because it is all we can see directly, and we have to use it as a guide to understanding the child. However, we must remember that these are really areas of development not actual behaviours. Each individual with an ASD may display very different behaviour, so it is not at this level we need to understand or work with the autism, although behaviour will be useful in determining individual differences.

The important area is the middle one, where the biology translates into behaviour, i.e. the psychological level. If we are to work effectively with children with ASDs, we must try to understand how they are thinking, learning, feeling, understanding, memorising, perceiving and so on. Of course we will have to use behaviour as a guide to all of this, but we will have to go beyond that to try to see what it means in terms of the way the child is understanding and functioning in the world.

Understanding the behaviour helps
As an example, consider the case of a three year-old boy (Tom), introduced to a mainstream nursery school setting on the advice of the health visitor because he appeared to be very unsociable, with very difficult behaviour at home (including very little sleep). Tom's parents had recently had a new baby, to which some of his difficulties were attributed, and were finding it increasingly difficult to manage. It was hoped that the nursery, which had a very good history of coping with 'difficult' and unruly toddlers, would help him regularise his behaviour and be able to offer support to the parents in how to manage his behaviour at home.

Tom appeared to be bright and could do many things for himself (including a 100 piece jigsaw puzzle – turning the pieces over so that the picture was hidden) but, although he had developed single words at the normal time and had short phrases (mostly from the television or the *Thomas the Tank Engine* videos which he insisted on watching over and over again), he now hardly spoke at all. He did not use speech to communicate and did not appear to listen to, still less obey, other people. Instead, he would drag and pull people to anything he could not get himself.

The nursery staff applied the good positive behavioural strategies that had been so effective with other disruptive children. They gave Tom his own star chart, and showed him that he could earn stars for 'good' behaviour (also highly verbally praised) and exchange them for special treats, such as the opportunity to watch his favourite *Thomas the Tank Engine* video. This seemed to work at first in that Tom got the 'hang' of the exchange, seemed to enjoy collecting the stars in themselves, but especially enjoyed exchanging them for his treat. However, although this regime increased the amount of 'good' responses he made, it seemed to do little to decrease his difficult behaviour. He was just as likely to leap up and rip something from the wall the moment after getting a star for 'sitting nicely', as before, and there were just as many instances of him pushing children over, kicking staff who tried to move him on from an activity (especially when that was ending his video watching treat) and biting or scratching children sitting on bikes he wanted or who happened to be near when he was upset for no easily discernible reason. In addition, he became obsessional about the stars, refusing to do anything without a star and showing no interest in the praise that was supposed to be gradually taking their place. In fact, he seemed to find the praise aversive, covering his ears and closing his eyes whenever he was praised and then having a violent temper tantrum if the praise was not followed by the star.

It is not that positive behavioural approaches are wrong in ASDs, just that we need to apply them in a more sophisticated way, which takes account of what underlies the behaviour and does not just deal with the behaviour itself. Praise is often meaningless in ASDs (at least in the early years) and can be counter-productive in that it may distract the child from what it is they are supposed to be doing or may even (as appeared to be the case with Tom) be punishing, because it is too loud or invasive. Tangible rewards like gold stars can appear very effective to begin with and can have a role when you need to break a difficult behaviour and train something else. However, the downside is, as here, that they become obsessional and eventually increase problems as the child's behaviour gets more and more dependent on these stars. It is better, in fact, to go for teaching routines as good work habits, rather than using rewards. Just knowing what is going to happen next and when a task will be finished, is rewarding for most children with ASDs, and is far easier to work with. Later chapters will give examples of easy visual 'work' schedules (using pictures or objects) that can be set up to give children like Tom the experience and understanding of 'work then play' where 'work' means something someone else wants you to do and 'play' is something you choose yourself, even if it does not look much like play to others.

Finally, it is important to remember that Tom is not 'choosing' to be difficult; he needs to be trained in how to conform, because he cannot 'pick up' what is expected from others, nor understand what it means to please others or be approved of. He does not enjoy all the trouble he gets into, although there is a danger that he may come to do so if it happens predictably enough or if people shouting and gesticulating is seen as interesting or funny. He simply is unable to inhibit his behaviours and so needs specific training in how to react to certain situations (like waiting for your turn on a bicycle) where at the moment his response is unacceptable. It is almost always a waste of time saying 'No' on its own; we must emphasise what it is he should do instead. Being shown visually when his turn is coming up and what he has to do before it comes up, will help him (and the rest of the nursery) cope with inevitable waiting times. However, Tom is unlikely to go from a stage of wanting whatever he wants immediately, to accepting having to wait his 'fair' turn. Explain to the other children that Tom does not know how to wait but is being trained and initially let him have a 'go' every other turn, gradually increasing the number of turns he has to wait (still giving him visual prompts for what he must do while waiting).

It is also difficult for children with ASDs to mark the passage of time so giving up the bike (or stopping watching the video) becomes a problem. A simple solution in the case of the bicycle is to have a 'task' associated with the bike time. Have a bag of ping-pong balls on the bike which are colour-coded to be posted at different areas round the playground. This gives interest and purpose to the 'ride' and clearly marks that when all the balls have gone, it is time for someone else to have a turn collecting them up.

Work or video tasks can be marked with a giant egg timer. The child is also more likely to conform if given warnings, and time to prepare him or herself for the change. Going up to Tom three minutes before the time to end an activity and saying, 'In three minutes it will be time to finish and ...' (whatever is next) and then repeating this at two and one minutes and finally saying, '*Now* it is time to finish and ...' usually works.

Secondary problems

A lot of the behaviour that is commonly seen in ASDs is secondary to the autism. Challenging behaviour, for example, arises from frustration at not being able to get needs met, or influence others, or from fear or panic. It is always dependent on the environment and so can be made considerably better by adjusting the environment. Certainly that is an easier task than trying to change the behavioural reaction, which even people without ASDs find very difficult to accomplish (think of things like changing diet or giving up smoking in yourself or someone you know).

It is always worth trying to teach in a positive way that will prevent many secondary problems arising. Teaching the child to play the same games as others may enable entry to a social group and so prevent social isolation. Teaching communication as early as possible may prevent much frustration. Teaching interaction in structured one-to-one sessions helps the child develop positive reactions to people, learn more about them and find them less unpredictable and frightening. Reducing stress is perhaps the single most important thing that can be done to enable the child to learn better and not to exhibit many of the secondary effects of stress. This can be done by:

- supporting the child (usually visually) through task demands;

- reducing spoken language;

- reducing the overall stimulation of the environment;

- providing a visual structure to help the child understand what is going on;

- giving the child a way of escaping when things get too much.

Compensatory behaviours

It may sometimes appear as if children with ASDs are being deliberately difficult or their behaviour may be a complete puzzle, or extremely bizarre. It should be remembered that, like us all, they are just trying to understand and 'get by' as best they can. All behaviour is serving some function for the child or it would not exist, no matter how obnoxious or strange it may seem. Often the behaviour is there to compensate for some missing behaviour, something not understood, or as a way of coping with some kind of stress. Self-injurious behaviour, like violent head banging or face slapping, for example, often arises as a reaction to unbearable levels of stimulation from noisy, over-lit classrooms with lots of talking and high demands, with no direct support. Of course, it may then attract attention and eventually come to be used when the child is bored and wants attention. Thus, teasing out the different functions of behaviour is a complex task, but it is one worth taking in the effort to understand the child.

Chapter Four

Educational goals and specialist approaches

The individual child

As with any child with special needs, the child with an ASD is a child first. As such s/he has the same entitlement to a broad and relevant curriculum, to develop potential to the full, as any other child. Children's special needs arise from the ASD and any accompanying condition, but also from their strengths and from the characteristics of the environment in which they are placed. Two children with very similar levels of disability in terms of their ASD and accompanying difficulties will nevertheless have very different outcomes if the pre-school services differ in terms of adaptability, understanding and degree of support, and if the home backgrounds are more or less supportive. It is important to know about the ASD, but it is just as important to know about how that is manifest in this particular individual and how far home and other environments are supportive of this child's development.

The child's needs have to be assessed on two fronts:

- what is needed to help the child overcome the problems arising from the ASD and thus reduce its impact on development;

- what is needed to help the child gain access to the teaching and learning opportunities available to other children and thus to prevent secondary problems arising.

The two aspects are not entirely independent, but it is important that we recognise these distinct aims of early years education, when applied to a child with an ASD. The first strand is the one most concentrated on by specific early interventions, with a goal of reducing the ASD. At the same time, UK educational legislation focuses on the second, with its emphasis on inclusion. This is the root of much misunderstanding between parents and professionals and it is helpful to recognise the validity of both approaches and to understand the goals of each.

Specific early interventions

The claims

Any concerned parent surfing the Internet will come across a bewildering array of interventions in ASDs, most making extravagent claims about their ability to transform the ASD and thus the prognosis for the child. These claims are backed up by 'first-hand' parental endorsements, some of which give accounts of their child's apparent transformation following this or that intervention. Many are very expensive and urge the parents to 'fight' for the right of their child to have this intervention, with the implication that the only reason professionals would not offer it is this cost. In addition, there may be assertions that more balanced or 'eclectic' (taken from more than one intervention or approach) methods will disadvantage the child by denying him or her the 'best' that is available and 'wasting' valuable learning time. It is not surprising, therefore, if parents become frantic in their efforts to obtain what they see as the best option for their child. This will be especially true where there is no good, coherent early years programme for ASDs in the area.

In turn, there will be similar pressure on early years practitioners to follow these interventions. Yet many are contradictory and, even with the best will and resources, it is difficult to know what to do. These 'information' sites are often little more than advertisements for particular interventions and need to be treated with the same caution as any other advertisement. Even where 'scientific' evidence is quoted, it is usually one-sided and critics are dismissed as 'ignorant' or malevolent. For professionals, the dangers are either of being completely caught up with the parents' enthusiasm or being completely cynical and ignoring potentially beneficial approaches. The ideal is to understand the basis of the claims made, assess when and for whom particular interventions may work, and apply that knowledge effectively in individual cases. There is the additional factor of needing to support parents and work with them, which may be the overriding consideration in many cases.

In the sections that follow, some of the most common special interventions for young children with ASDs are described. Many have something valuable to offer, which may help a particular child at a particular point. However, this does not mean that the interventions mentioned are of particular value to all or that others, not mentioned, may not be as useful. I have chosen those which early years practitioners are likely to come across, with the aim of helping practitioners select for themselves those aspects they wish to pursue.

Reviews of research on these interventions have shown that there is promising evidence of effectiveness in a few, but none are successful with all children and there is no good evidence that one is better than others (Jordan et al., 1998; Dawson & Osterling, 1997). Children with ASDs are very different from one another, in spite of what they also have in common, so it is not surprising that one approach will not suit all. In addition, the interventions often set out to do very different things so the one that is 'best' will depend very much on what your goals are, and these may vary with the activity or with the stage the child has reached. Thus, even for a particular child, there is seldom a single intervention that is suited to all aspects of development, and a good eclectic approach is the best way forward. However, this means that practitioners need to know something about all these interventions and their potential, if suitable choices are to be made.

Behavioural approaches

These often have the highest profile with parents because of the way they are promoted. They may be labelled as ABA (Applied Behaviour Analysis) or intensive behavioural therapy or be named after one of the proponents (Lovaas being the most likely). They have been used with children with ASDs since the 1960s, when they were the most common method of teaching any child or adult with learning difficulties in the UK as well as the USA. They are characterised by:

- a positive approach – any child can be worked with;

- breaking tasks down into small steps;

- teaching the steps one at a time (often starting with the last step first – a process called 'backward chaining' – so the child was always rewarded by completing the task);

- use of prompting;

- shaping of the child's responses;

- tangible rewards (often food);

- sessions firmly teacher-directed;

- child having to reach set criteria of correct performance on one step before progressing to the next;

- unwanted behaviours reduced or eliminated by application of the same behavioural principles – rewarding prompted alternatives and punishing the unwanted response;

- good recording of baseline behaviours and outcome measures.

Initial satisfaction with these methods diminished in the 1980s in the UK when it was found that behaviour taught in this way often failed to generalise and continued to need very specific prompting throughout life. There were also problems in the general revulsion to (and then illegality of) using aversives (shouts, slaps, lemon juice squirted into the mouth and so on) and the fact than many hundreds of hours were being spent with often trivial results in terms of the person's quality of life. Other approaches gained ground but the study that brought these methods back into favour was the Young Autism Project (Lovaas, 1987; McEachin et al., 1993). This programme applied ABA techniques intensively (40+ hours a week) to pre-school children with autism for a period of at least two years, with a parallel programme of getting the child into a mainstream nursery setting and training the child beforehand to succeed in that placement. Aversives were used (although they are not now used in any of the current programmes) and the results were remarkable. Almost half the group (as compared to only one of the 'control' children who received up to ten hours of ABA per week) were said to have achieved 'normal functioning' by age seven years, and in most cases this was sustained at 13 years.

For a critique of the research on this (and other approaches), see Jordan et al. (1998). However, even allowing for these problems, the results claimed were better than anything that has been seen before or since. Attempts to replicate this finding, however, have not yet been successful, especially when done in more natural community settings. Nearly all cases that use ABA report some worthwhile gains in children's skills and in the reduction of challenging behaviour, although there are also cases where children appear adversely affected after a time. There has been no good research to discover:

- who the children are who most benefit from this approach;

- whether positive results are from the particular programme or just from its intensity;

- what level of intensity is needed;

- what role the integrated experience had in the success of the original programme, as opposed to the ABA itself.

There seems enough case study evidence to suggest that behavioural methods such as these have a role to play in the early education of children with ASDs (as all public enquiries and reviews have noted), but how big a role is open to question. A worrying aspect of the marketing of ABA approaches is the insistence that parents do nothing else. ABA techniques would be useful for teachers to be acquainted with, since they have a role with many children in the training of certain basic habits (such as good hygiene or dressing skills). However, if it were used exclusively for any long period of time there are dangers in the child not understanding any better, but just learning to perform automatically. Nevertheless, some systematic training in basic skills can only help the child gain access to other learning, and the principle of targeting key behaviours that will enable interaction with other children is a good one. The sections written by parents in Keenan et al. (2000) are a good guide to what ABA programmes are like and can achieve, although the book is marred by the denigration of other approaches and of anyone who voices a word of caution.

TEACCH

This stands for Treatment and Education of Autistic and Communication-impaired Children (Mesibov, 1997; Schopler & Mesibov, 1995). It was started in North Carolina in the 1960s and has been exported to most countries in the world. Its principles are:

- an individual approach;

- based on detailed assessment;

- the creation of a learning environment and teaching methods best adapted to the child's learning style;

- working with parents as co-therapists;

- providing a 'cradle to grave' support system for individuals with ASDs and their families.

In the UK it is best known for its emphasis on visually supported instruction and structured teaching through which the child will be 'told' by the organisational structure:

- what to do;

- when;

- with whom;

- where;

- when the task is finished;

- what to do next.

Mostly these are in the form of pictorial (or for young children perhaps object-focused) timetables (individually based) and work systems where good work habits (work left to right, top to bottom, work then play and so on) are taught. Watson et al. (1989) and Peeters (1997) give good practical examples of how to use these TEACCH-based schedules, and other examples appear in this book.

Where there have been evaluations of TEACCH, all show very positive, but not remarkable, results. Its worldwide success suggests that it is meeting the needs of children, parents and professionals for a teaching approach that is based on adaptation to the child and to the environment. Its research base does not come from outcome studies but from evidence of the way that individuals with autism think and learn, and it is continually adapting as new evidence emerges.

The actual teaching methods used in one-to-one sessions in TEACCH are behaviourally based in that the teacher sets the agenda but, rather than rewarding correct responses with edibles, the child is taught 'work then play' sequences whereby more favoured activities reinforce less favoured (or new) ones. There is also an emphasis on teaching the child to finish a piece of work and the children are trained to do so independently. Any 'rewards' used are functional to the task, and social rewards such as praise are also kept to social situations or they tend to disrupt the work pattern. Children are taught new tasks one-to-one with the teacher, then they are taught to practise them independently and to speed up their performance, while maintaining accuracy (this can be done with games such as 'beating' a giant timer). This makes generalisation easier since the skill is now fluent and at this stage they then learn to do the task with others in social settings.

Within the task, there are visual guides which help the child focus attention appropriately, and the child may be working at a 'work station' in which noise and visual distraction is minimised. This may be a formal 'booth' or it may just be in a corner with a temporary screen and a blank wall. This setting recognises the difficulty in selecting out relevant information from displays or where there are windows or other children to distract. In social sessions the child may be given little picture strips to show the 'rules' of the session and (by matching his/her own card to the right place) the child learns to wait, to take turns and to tolerate sitting in a group because s/he understands the structure of what is happening (it is spelt out in the picture strip) and when it will come to an end.

Interactive methods
As the name suggests, these focus on building up the child's understanding of, and enjoyment from, interaction with others. Normally developing children learn a myriad of skills and attitudes to learning within

early lap play and interaction 'games' with caregivers. In interactions, the child learns:

- the timing of two-way interaction;

- how to take turns;

- mutual imitation;

- sharing in the emotions of the adults;

- self and other awareness;

- a sense of agency;

- joint attention;

- monitoring the eye gaze and actions of others;

- careful attunement to others;

- modulation of own level of arousal to match the level of involvement of the caretaker.

In order for all this important learning to take place, and these early interactions to be successful, the baby has to be innately endowed with the capacity to respond to interaction signals.

It is the latter that is missing or disturbed in autism. This means the early interactions with caregivers are at best unsatisfactory and often hardly take place at all. This is not because the mother is neglectful in any sense, but because the child is unresponsive and, without that response, it is very difficult (at least without considerable support) for mothers and others to continue with the interaction. Right from the beginning, therefore, many children with ASDs are missing out on just the opportunities for learning that they most need, and thus further damaging their capacity to understand and get along with others. Interactive methods mirror the same learning opportunities as the normally developing child experiences as a baby, but in a way from which the child with an ASD can benefit. Sometimes (as in the Option/Son Rise programme: Kaufman, 1994) this is done intensively, as a way of preparing the child for later learning. The belief is that establishing a relationship with others is a necessary first step to learning. Other interventions (the Interaction Curriculum: Nind & Hewett, 1994; Hewett & Nind, 1998; Communication Interaction: Christie et al., 1992; Chandler et al., 2002; or Hanen: Sussman, 1999) form just a part of the child's programme with skill-based learning also having a part.

Common to these approaches are:
- a slowing down of the interaction;

- exaggeration of the cues that tell the child when it is his/her turn to communicate (such as the rising intonation and the expectant pause);

- giving the child longer to respond;

- use of a play format;

- allowing (at least initially) the child to lead the interaction;

- picking up on the child's behaviour as the basis for an interaction sequence, even if the child is clearly not intending the action as communicative;

- helping the child focus on the adult and the interaction in some way. Often the interaction programme will take place in a distraction-free (or reduced) setting with very few props or toys, so that the adult becomes the main focus for the child. Some programmes use a live musician or the adult singing to provide a structure to the social interaction and to emphasise key features for the child;

- no external rewards and no 'right' way to respond;

- aim to help children with ASDs enjoy being with others;

- teaching of key interactive skills;

- using taught interactive skills as a basis for learning other skills with the same adult.

There are only case study reports of success but staff and parents, especially at the pre-school level, find this method of working with the young child very rewarding, and report a high degree of satisfaction. However, most parents do want to move onto skill teaching at some point and few are happy to have this as the total programme beyond the earliest years. Nevertheless, parents may develop new ways of relating to their own child successfully through these methods, enabling them to be 'in contact' with, and enjoying, their child, perhaps for the first time.

Cognitive approaches

The rationale for cognitive approaches in ASDs is that the child does not have a normal natural understanding of self and others and has to 'work it out' (cognitively). These approaches, then, use these children's natural strengths to address their weaknesses, but they require some professional understanding of thinking and learning processes and so they are not so well developed as approaches that require less training (Powell & Jordan, 1994). Nevertheless, they may appeal to early years staff in that one programme uses the structure of the High Scope nursery programme (Schweinhart & Weikart, 1997). This has some shortcomings for the child with an ASD (Jordan & Powell, 1990) but has been adapted as a pre-school cognitive programme (Bright Start – Schopler & Mesibov, 1995), teaching the child to:

• make choices and plan;

• be aware of themselves and their learning as they learn;

• review (or, preferably, reflect) on their learning afterwards.

It can incorporate some elements of the TEACCH programme into this process.

A cognitive approach is also the best umbrella for approaches that specifically teach the child with an ASD to play, by scaffolding the child's responses (Schuler & Wolfberg, 2000) and developing pretend play (Beyer & Gammeltoft, 2000; Jordan, 2001; Libby et al., 1998; Sherratt & Peter, 2002). Play development will be dealt with in later chapters. It is important to teach play in the early years because children with ASDs will not come to it spontaneously and it is a rich source of learning (Jordan & Libby, 1997; Sherratt & Peter, 2002).

Finally, in this section, comes the role of information and communication technology (ICT). Murray (1997) has made a passionate case for the importance of ICT in the learning of individuals with ASDs, and this has potential at the pre-school stage, as at others. One has only to look at the fascinations of young children with ASDs, to see some of this potential. They love repetition because of the opportunities it gives them to predict, and potentially control, their environment and because it provides maximum opportunity to learn and make sense of their learning. Many families are driven wild by the child with an ASD's insistence on the same piece of video played endlessly again and again, but one family has capitalised on this obsession and used their own video learning opportunities for their child (with the added advantage of using the little boy's sister in an enjoyable way, to help her brother: A to Z method by video: National Autistic Society). There are very useful games at the pre-school level which provide educational opportunities for learning to attend, respond to signals, problem solve, gain success and, best of all, be able to share their enjoyment and success with others. Autism and Computing (a London-based organisation) has a video that shows a resourceful family with three children with ASDs (as well as two without) and how fun at the computer helps them all to share learning and fun opportunities together.

Daily Life Therapy
This is better known by the names of the schools (the original in Tokyo, then Boston and now, under another name, in the UK) in which it is practised: the Higashi schools. It originated in Japan (Kitahara, 1984) and is based on principles derived from primary school education in Japan:

- a clear structure with demarcated areas, times for activities, and clear signals for starting and finishing;

- a 24-hour curriculum that focuses on the early developmental skills of dressing, feeding, control of the body, good sleep and exercise patterns, attention to 'teacher' and group conformity;

39

- a 'whole person' view of education that includes body and mind in harmony through physical, academic, daily living and aesthetic activities;

- group rather than personal success, and an age-appropriate academic curriculum (achieved through physical guidance) without concern for developmental relevance.

There is little scientific evidence of long-term benefit, beyond what would be expected from a highly concentrated programme over 24 hours, often from a young age. Nevertheless, the structure of the activities, the role of aerobic physical exercise in modulating behaviour and the benefits of an intensive skills-based 24-hour curriculum all have evidence of positive outcomes in ASDs. Parents certainly report satisfaction and the improvement in behaviour and basic 'learning to attend' skills that would be predicted. Against this, there is little evidence of individualised programming to meet individual educational plans (even where these exist) and many children seem patently unable to benefit academically from the level of lessons presented.

However, many schools for children with ASDs in the UK have recognised the benefit to be gained from the physical activities in particular and have adapted their presentation for a UK context. There is also a lot to be gained from the way in which the structure of lessons is clearly signalled (often by a whistle and lining up in Japan), which may seem curiously 'old-fashioned' but has great appeal to young children, and children with ASDs in particular. The clear focus of activities (Jordan et al.,1999) is also valuable: for example, not allowing the fact that the child drops the paint container on the floor to distract from the goal of getting the child to transport the container for him/herself to the easel. Thus, there is no change of focus for the child as the pot drops, rather another pot is given immediately, while someone else attends to the clearing up of the mess. On the other hand, the child is not allowed to distract either. The child painting his/her hands, while meant to be painting a particular picture, will be given no opportunity to enjoy the sensuality of the paint on the hand or explore hand painting at this point, but will immediately have the paint washed away (without any remonstration or verbal redirection) and be directed physically once more to the task. All this takes extremely vigilant and hardworking staff, but does enable children with ASDs to learn to conform (and understand) teacher demands in a way that is otherwise very difficult for them.

As this account makes apparent, there are also some problems with this approach when used in its entirety. Most Western staff would not be happy to ignore relevance to the child's developmental level or their capacity to understand what they were being taught. The methods used are more physical than most early years practitioners would feel comfortable with or be skilled in using. The degree of staff involvement in continually physically 'refocusing' the child, to prevent stereotypies and to promote on-task behaviour, is again something that would require a certain level of staff resources and staff training to achieve. As with other approaches, however, there are aspects (especially the emphasis on physical activity and control) that are of great benefit in the early years. It is also an approach that teaches 'skills' that parents most appreciate (apart from communication, which is not emphasised): toileting, control, sleeping, feeding and learning to wait.

Putting it together

Later chapters will explore other specific interventions to develop social understanding, communication and language. This chapter has just introduced the main kinds of specific interventions that the pre-school child may be exposed to, or that pre-school environments may be thinking of incorporating. As implied, there are a lot of advantages in trying to build on the best from each approach to construct a curriculum best adapted to each individual, while also recognising the cultural context of the setting, which in England and Wales will include the National Curriculum. There are also some dangers. Those who advocate sticking to single approaches point to the difficulties of staff understanding all the approaches, and risking a superficial and, ultimately, perhaps unsatisfactory adoption of any approach. They also suggest that some approaches are fundamentally contradictory (for example over the issue of whether the learning is adult or child-led) and the child will be confused by switching from one to another, to the possible detriment of both.

These are real dangers and need positive strategies to avoid them. Staff need primarily to understand ASDs and not just one intervention technique; they need to understand each child's learning needs. Then they need a thorough training in the methods to be adopted, so that they understand the principles behind them and can adapt them to suit their own circumstances. An uncritical three-day training is unlikely to give that thorough understanding, unless there is local expertise to offer sustained support and guidance during the implementation stage. Staff also need to understand how to structure learning environments to indicate clearly, for example, when the child is to be 'in control' of a session and when it is 'teacher's turn' to dictate the structure. Both have their place in ASDs, but it is vital that they are not confused.

Staff also need, sadly, even at the pre-school stage, to be given permission to enjoy their time with the children, by emphasis on the importance of this to the learning of children with ASDs. Teaching children with ASDs gives you a crucial opportunity to re-evaluate your teaching of all children and to reassert the values and goals that most of us believe should be at the heart of education.

Chapter Five

Working with parents

Importance of parent partnership in ASDs

'Parent partnership' is particularly important when working with children with ASDs in the early years. For all other children, including those with other special needs, the child will have basic skills of social interaction and communication, or will acquire these, without specific teaching. However, the child with an ASD will need to be taught these basic ways of understanding and dealing with the world: how to 'read' the social and emotional messages of others and how to develop his/her own ways of communicating and being with others. That kind of learning and teaching cannot be confined to academic sessions in a professional setting, but must be part of everyday life. Parents need to understand their own child, just as staff do, and they need to know how to use everyday opportunities to support their child in reaching a better understanding of the world.

Thus, parents and early years staff need to pool knowledge and understanding of the child and to produce agreed ways forward that will cover both home and school. That is not to say that parents have to behave like teachers, or turn home into a classroom, quite the reverse. The child-centred atmosphere of a home, where important needs are naturally met, is often the best context for the introduction of much of this basic teaching. Thus, it is often better if roles are reversed (in some areas at least) and the school staff work to generalise and extend what has been started at home.

Parents, too, may not just need support, but be in a position to offer support. Often they are the ones with more opportunities to attend conferences, read and hear more about ASDs, than early years staff. They may be the ones to lend books and videos to staff to keep them informed and tell them about local conferences or meetings they may wish to attend. They can also be a powerful political ally for staff who are seeking additional resources for the child with the ASD.

There will also be situations where parents are not so well informed and may not even be ready to accept the diagnosis. Or it may be that they have had to fight to get recognition that something was wrong with their child, and/or to try to get what they feel would be best (whether or not that is true, does not matter in terms of parental perception). Others may have tried something and it has not worked as they hoped. For all these reasons, and many more, parents may feel angry and bitter and this is often directed at early years staff (at least initially) just because they are there. This is understandable, but in the child's best interests, staff will have to work harder to build the trust upon which parent partnership depends.

Particular concerns of parents of children with ASDs

Almost all parents want to do what is best for their child, although they may not always concur with professionals. However, parents of children with ASDs face particular challenges and have particular concerns which make them more vulnerable to unscrupulous marketing, more anxious to try 'anything' and more suspicious of professional advice. Some of the reasons for this are:

- The strong genetic link in ASDs means some parents may share some difficulties in processing information in a social context (they may prefer a booked telephone call or a letter/email as a way of 'talking through' an issue, for example). It also means they may have anxieties about other current or future children or feel devastated that it is 'their' gene that has done this, even though it is not their 'fault' in any rational sense. This can make them prickly and defensive when there are comments about the child's behaviour at home or relationships with siblings and so on. Staff need to be sensitive to this.

- All other disabilities (except progressive diseases), no matter how severe, offer the comfort to parents of being able to help and support their child. Once parents have got over their initial grief at the 'loss' of the perfect child they hoped for, they usually take on a practical role, working hard to try to minimise the effect of the disability and to help their child lead as normal and fulfilled a life as possible. Parents of children with ASDs have these same needs and reactions but the difference is that they do not know how to help their child. Often it is very difficult to understand and accept the nature of this devastating condition in a child who appears to be so healthy. The very 'natural' things they try to do to help their child are often rebuffed or appear to make things worse, and the parents are left feeling frustrated, helpless and desperate. Sadly, they often find the professionals they turn to equally bemused, so it is not surprising if they then turn to someone (or something) that apparently has all the answers.

• Effective ways of relating to children with ASDs do not come naturally; they need to be trained. The nature of the disorder is such that the child cannot respond naturally to the normal social and emotional cues, so just repeating them is frustrating for everyone concerned. Parents need to be taught how to respond to their child and how to 'read' his or her behaviour. We have to remember that ASDs are transactional disorders. You can pick up that a child has an ASD by the way he/she makes you feel as you try to interact with him/her. For professionals this can be bad enough, when your normal ways of making a relationship with a child have no effect and you feel at a loss as to how to move on from there. Imagine how much worse this is for parents when it feels like a very personal rejection and a devastating failure to get through to your child.

Parent training

Many pre-school programmes train parents, either to work directly with their child on the programme or to manage volunteers or paid workers who come into the home to work with the child. Mostly these programmes just train the parents to follow one approach, although there may be some information about some aspects of ASDs and the rationale for the particular programme being used. This section concentrates on programmes whose rationale is not direct work with the child but empowerment of parents to do so. Many local health, educational or even joint initiatives in the UK have developed their own pre-school visiting services for parents of children with ASDs. Some of these use highly trained and knowledgeable staff and offer a very effective service. Some will use named programmes, some will develop their own. Sometimes this is offered alongside a nursery school placement, sometimes as a precursor to it. The National Initiative for Autism: Screening and Assessment (NIASA) is a body set up to make recommendations about diagnostic and early intervention services in the UK and recommends the establishment of such services as an entitlement in all areas.

Below are some named programmes, which may be part of this early intervention and parental support package:

- *EarlyBird* (Shields, 2001)
  This is a parent training programme set up by the National Autistic Society, using elements from a number of other programmes. It follows a structure of one day a week group training for parents over a ten-week period with two home visits in which sessions with the parents and child are videod, watched together and commented on. Parents are given a manual containing information and strategies. The content of the sessions is understanding ASDs, using visually supported training of basic skills (from TEACCH), using a PECS programme to teach communication, learning a functional approach to managing behaviour and learning the Hanen (Sussman, 1999) form of interaction with a child where the adult learns to OWL (Observe – Wait – Listen). Parental reports are very positive and the programme is being evaluated more formally.

- *Home-visiting schemes*
  These may be run by local educational authorities (when it is often a visiting teacher service or a specialist nursery nurse), or health authorities (when it might be a specialist health visitor, speech and language therapist or clinical psychologist). Sometimes there is joint funding for these and sometimes a social worker may be involved – especially in liaising with the family over benefits and dealing with general family support issues. In some areas these visits involve systematic parent training, perhaps using schemes such as ***Portage*** (an ASD adapted version) where parents are given weekly developmental targets to work on with their children. Other schemes are less formal and offer only general support and advice. Good practice would be liaison between this home-visiting support and any nursery or early

years setting the child may be attending, but this does not always happen. It is important that staff of early years centres ask about such schemes so that they can help parents set priorities, ensure that they are not being given conflicting advice and that too many demands are not being made. Parents may be very reluctant to turn down any offer of help for their child, but can become overwhelmed, if this is not managed sensitively for them.

- *Early social communication programmes*
  This includes **Hanen** (Sussman, 1999), **Child Talk** (Aldred, 2002) and **Communication Training** (Chandler et al., 2002). The foci of these are on teaching parents how to best work with their child to encourage communication, social interaction and language. The Hanen programme has the structure as described under EarlyBird above, while the other two depend on home visits, supported by video analysis in the same way as Hanen, and training materials. All three programmes have recently been evaluated against progress of a comparison group of children, although the Hanen evaluation is multi-site and is not yet complete. The other approaches show positive results of the programme.

Parent support

Parents need to be kept informed of their child's day-to-day progress and should be involved in planning and implementing IEPs, reviews and their child's daily programme. This can all work well when the child is making good progress, but it can be harder to support parents when the child regresses for any reason or his/her behaviour deteriorates. It is then that the trust between parents and staff is most tested so it is important to nurture this trust on a daily basis.

- *Home-school diaries*
  These can be a valuable way of keeping in touch or they can be a source of stress for staff and anxiety for parents. It will not help trust if staff keep things from parents, but equally it will depress parents, if each day is full of negative statements about the child. There should be two positive statements at least for each negative one and even negative ones can be phrased positively. It helps no one just to be told

that the child has done something terrible, but parents can feel reassured if staff report why they think it happened and what they are doing to make sure it does not happen again. It is natural and appropriate for staff to ask parents questions to try to get a better picture of what is happening at home, but they should be sensitive to parents interpreting this as trying to 'blame' them for their child's difficulties or suggesting that they are not coping. Thus, instead of something like:

Johnny had a temper tantrum that lasted 20 minutes in school today, where he knocked over tables and chairs, screamed and hit himself. Does he have these at home?

which is calculated to alarm parents, you might write about the incident thus:

Johnny reacted very badly today when another child took a Thomas train he had been playing with. By the time we were able to restore the train he was inconsolable, and his distress and anger lasted about 20 minutes. We have talked about it and agreed a programme of helping Johnny on two fronts. First we will teach him to give us a 'help' symbol when he needs an adult to intervene on his behalf, and secondly we will work on his toleration of others sharing in his Thomas games (each with their own engine at first, of course!). We wondered if you had any strategies to share with us about how to help Johnny manage to avoid these upsets and how to calm him down once it has happened?

This way, the outburst is reported honestly, but in a much more positive vein and parental support is asked for, with less chance of misinterpretation.

• Home-school books are also good opportunities to bridge the gap between home and school for the child as well as the adults. After activities, plan for an extra ten minutes or so to go through the activity with the child, using miniature pictures, symbols or written words, as appropriate. By sticking these symbols in the home-school book with the child, it gives you the chance to stress to the child that we need to 'tell' mummy and daddy what we have been doing in school because they are not there. Then at home, the parents have a very concrete record of what the child has done. They can go through the symbols, reinforcing the learning, helping to generalise it and feeling part of their child's education.

- *Difficult behaviour*
One source of tension between home and school is when the child is showing extremely difficult behaviour in one context only. When the challenging behaviour is only seen at home, the implication often made is that this is because of the relative lack of skill of parents in dealing with it. The school or centre staff may be very sympathetic, well aware of the extra pressures of living with a problem for 24 hours a day, seven days a week, and they may make good suggestions for additional ways to train or support parents. They may be right that it is the comparative lack of skill in handling the behaviour that has led to the difference, but it is extremely unlikely. Most parents are very skilful at handling their own child, although the round of sleepless nights and stress may take its toll. If parents are seeking additional support and training, then it should be provided, but, before assuming that is the reason, staff need to look at the overall pattern of the child's day.

A child will often settle well into an early years centre, only for staff to find that parents report a great increase in disturbed and challenging behaviour at home. It is unlikely that parents have suddenly become less competent, so the most likely explanation for the change in behaviour at home is that it is a reaction to the centre. For example, a young boy may be apparently managing his new 'school' but coping with it on a daily basis is causing him anxiety and stress. This builds up in his time at school but it is not revealed until he gets home when the slightest amount of additional stress (perhaps just having to deal with greetings from parents or siblings) is enough to send him over the top. If this seems a reasonable hypothesis for what is going on, then the remedy is to look at the entire day to try to reduce stress, not just the period at home.

The first obvious sources of stress are too much social contact, too many demands and too much noise or confusion. Try to reduce these as far as possible. You could introduce a period of vigorous exercise at some point in the day to help the child get rid of some of the accumulated stress before going home. You could also introduce a relaxation time in which all the children are taught to relax – good for all children, as well as staff. You could reduce lighting, let the children lie on mats, play soothing music, spray some lavender water around and perhaps introduce some simple tensing and relaxing games or some gentle massage. When you find something that seems to work for the child you could tell the parents about it so they might try it – perhaps as a way of preparing the child for sleep.

Less commonly, we get the situation in reverse. In this scenario, the boy has had little or no sleep (many young children with ASDs have sleep disturbance), little or no breakfast (food fads are a problem) and has had problems dressing (it is often difficult getting them to perform tasks to time). By the time he reaches school he is highly stressed from sleep deprivation, low blood sugar and frustration at being 'hassled' to get dressed on time. In this case it may be the key worker, or an unsuspecting child, who gets attacked, just for being in the wrong place at the wrong time. Sometimes, starting the day with a little 'breakfast' is a pleasant way of getting the children to join together and can raise blood sugar levels for the start of work (also, often appreciated by staff).

The point is, there is no simple answer to why a child (any child, but particularly one with an ASD) is behaving in a particular way. Parents and staff need to work together to suggest reasons and work out solutions, as far as possible, across both settings.

• *Respite and leisure care*
When a child is little, parents expect to have to provide 24-hour care, so it is sometimes assumed that having a young child with an ASD will make little difference to the burden on the family. This is to ignore the quite extraordinary stress on a family such a child may

cause (Randall & Parker, 1999), even without the likely problems of hyperactivity (often literally climbing up the walls, out of the windows and across the roofs), impulsivity (switching lights – and fire alarms – on and off, on and off, running out into the road, continually tapping, flicking, twisting) and destructiveness (unpicking clothes, bedding, curtains, unscrewing anything and everything, pulling off wallpaper, posters).

Parents need help with managing this behaviour, for which there are many more opportunities at home, but they also need some time to be with other children, to be together as a couple and to have some time for themselves. Even where befriending schemes have been set up, parents will still need positive encouragement to use them 'just' to have a good time. We all need some time off, and parents of children with ASDs, who need it most, are least likely to get the opportunity from support provided by family and friends. Grandparents and family friends may not understand the problems the family face, may even blame the family for the way the child behaves, or may not feel confident in looking after a child with such unusual and extreme behaviour. Thus, these families are often in desperate need of volunteer (trained) or professional family support services to provide opportunities to recharge batteries. Early years staff have a role in helping parents find, and then encouraging parents to take up, these opportunities.

Sibling support

Most research shows that brothers and sisters of children with ASDs do not show long-term ill effects from the undoubted stresses and difficulties of their childhood, often developing a strong sense of social justice and going into the caring professions themselves. Nevertheless, there are costs, and many have to grow up too quickly, shoulder burdens of care inappropriate to their age or watch with extreme distress as home (and even parents) are attacked. At times, they may be attacked themselves and some report being terrified of their brother or sister with the ASD at some time in their lives. At the very least, their lives are often restricted with family outings ruined or abandoned, being ashamed to bring friends into the home, having no peace to study or practise hobbies and often being teased or bullied at school on behalf of their sibling with the ASD. Clearly, there are needs for support in a number of different ways:

- *Time and space*
  Providing respite care to the child with an ASD will give siblings breathing space and the time and opportunity to do 'normal' family activities. Parents may need help in seeing that allowing a brother or sister to have some 'defended' space of their own is not an exclusion of the child with the ASD, but a way of enabling all the children to co-exist, protecting the rights of all.

- *Information*
  As for us all, it helps brothers and sisters if they understand why their sibling behaves as s/he does and there are now a number of good texts for all ages that explain about ASDs simply and well. Older children may benefit from reading some accounts of people with ASDs themselves, to help them understand further, and there are a few books by brothers or sisters. Some support organisations and some health authorities run sibling support groups, part of whose function is to give information. Older siblings may also welcome the opportunity to talk about the genetics of ASDs and to discuss their personal worries and concerns in relation to that.

- *Support and fun*
  Brothers and sisters of children with ASDs differ just as the children with ASDs themselves differ, but most welcome at least occasional opportunities to get together with other siblings of children with ASDs. This may have a counselling element, but there is no evidence of the need for formal counselling, beyond the opportunity to share experiences with others who understand and to express hurt, anger and some bitterness in a safe environment where parents do not need to know and where the pain can be resolved. However, they also welcome the opportunity to play together and can even enjoy playing with their brother or sister with an ASD within the supportive framework of others in the same situation who understand.

Chapter Six

Building communication

The nature of the problem

There are many reasons why children have difficulties learning to speak. Most early years staff will be used to dealing with children at a pre-linguistic level, making themselves understood and learning to understand the way the child is communicating. However, ASDs present a new challenge, even to experienced early years staff. Autistic conditions are the only ones where language and communication take separate developmental routes.

Thus, a young child with an ASD may have no spoken language, or s/he may have an advanced vocabulary and very sophisticated (adult-sounding) speech patterns. Yet in neither case will they have any understanding of communication. For non-speaking children, this means they will have developed no compensatory gestures or signs and their attempts to 'communicate' appear to be little more than treating people like objects to get things for them that they cannot get for themselves. Even children with good language skills may not be able to understand much language (certainly not if spoken to at the same speed and length of sentence at which they are speaking). They will not have any gestures, nor understand the gestures of others, and will not know how to use their language skills to communicate with others.

Language and communication

Autism teaches us that language is not always 'a form of communication' so in working with young children with ASDs we have to be prepared to teach both language and communication. 'Language' usually means a verbal language, either spoken or written, but it can mean a sign language as used by deaf communities. The processes of developing language and communication are complex. Most early years staff, working with children with ASDs, should be working alongside a speech and language therapist

(SLT) with expertise in ASDs. Their role is to help early years staff make the appropriate assessments and plan and monitor the programmes put in place. There is no point in SLTs working in isolation with children with ASDs, although some parents may believe that this is what 'speech and language therapy' means and may press for their child to have individual time with the SLT. That can be useful, especially at the beginning, to assess the child's understanding and formal production, but the child needs to understand about communication in real meaningful contexts, or any skill will remain an isolated 'trick'. SLTs need to work across home and school settings to monitor the agreed programme and to maximise the child's opportunities to learn.

Something to communicate *about*

The first thing a child needs in order to communicate is to have something to communicate about, that is, the child must have needs and wants. Children with ASDs have these, but may have little awareness of them, at least when young. If they do not know they want something, they cannot learn to communicate what they want to others. Equally, if the child's concepts (ideas about the world) are very different from others', staff will not be able to understand what the child is trying to 'say' and again communication will fail. Teaching about communication, therefore, must start at the beginning and help the child to have joint attention with others so they share a common view. Forms of interactive play (as mentioned in Chapter Four) will help with this.

Start by imitating the child in such a way that s/he notices, and then begin to vary the pace of imitation so the child is waiting for it and beginning to appreciate (and even enjoy) the turn-taking. Once that is established introduce some variations and try to entice the child to start imitating you. Once you have that, you have the start of joint attention, at least to your actions.

The next step is to get the children to understand the purpose of eye contact. It is no use just training children to look at you, if they do not know why they are looking nor how to make and break eye contact appropriately.

Being made to look at people who are speaking to them often means they get such an upsurge of levels of arousal that they may not be able to hear the person, so that is also counter-productive. What is important is to help them understand. A good start is to romp with a child, spinning him/her round and round, and then stop abruptly. If this is abrupt enough, even children with ASDs will usually look at the adult to see what has stopped him/her 'working'. As the child looks, you say, 'Oh! Would you like some more?' and twirl the child again. Eventually, the child connects the fact that his/her look is the signal for you to continue and will start using eye gaze as a communicative signal. Once that is achieved, the next step is to get the child to recognise your use of eye gaze as a signal. This is best done by explicitly letting your looking at the child be a signal for the child being allowed to have a 'turn' at something they like. You can tell when a child has understood this by the way s/he will seek out eye contact in those sessions.

Finally, you need to help children with ASDs understand what they are feeling, in situations where you are certain what this is (you do not want to mislabel an emotion and thereby further confuse a child). In this connection, you need to be very careful before singing, 'If you're happy and you know it ...' with a child who is patently far from happy, as is often the case. Look for clear situations of happiness, fear, anger and so on and then help the child know what they are feeling, as well as what led to it, and how you want them to express it (in the case of negative emotions which might otherwise lead to challenging behaviour).

Something to communicate *with*

A child who is not speaking needs to be given some way of communicating. Children with speech may also need a simpler system of pictures or symbols to help their expression when they are unable to find speech readily (especially if they are in the grip of a strong emotion like anger or fear). Parents in particular will often worry that if a child is given an alternative system to speech, they will rely on that and speech may not develop. This is an understandable but groundless fear. Of course, speech should still be worked on, but all the evidence shows that having *any* system of communication helps, not hinders, the development of speech.

There remain problems in deciding on the best system. There is no single answer and the best programmes vary what is used, depending on the child's needs and abilities and the contexts of communication. (See Table 6.1 below).

System	Precursors needed	Adaptation by others	Contexts of use
Physically manipulates others	None – sees others as 'tools' of own agency	None – but no real communication	Pushes or pulls someone to get co-operation
Objects of reference	Association of object with item/event or activity	Key others will need to learn the child's objects	Daily activities and to make key requests
Photographs/ realistic pictures	Association of picture with item/ event/activity	No special training needed	Any item, activity or event that can be pictured
Symbol systems (e.g.PECS*/ Makaton)	Association of symbol with item/ event/activity	Others will need training in the system	Anything that can be symbolised
Sign systems and gestures	Association of sign with item/ event/activity	Gestures none, signs – others need training	Signing for meaning in everyday environments
Written language (and by computer)	Reading vocabulary for items/events/ activities	None needed beyond reading ability	Where writing or computer use possible
Spoken language	Vocal output and understanding communication	None needed	All

Table 6.1 Augmentative systems of communication

*PECS stands for Picture Exchange Communication System (Bondy & Frost, 1994); Makaton is another symbol system tied into a signing system (Walker, 1980)

There are several things to note in Table 6.1. First of all, these systems are not listed in a developmental order of difficulty, although speech is clearly the most difficult and objects of reference the easiest of the true communication systems. Within these boundaries, however, some children with ASDs will find it far easier to learn symbols, or even written language, than to understand realistic pictures or photographs. Symbols seem to help a child focus on the essential features of an item or event whereas a photograph or picture may have too much distracting detail, making it hard for the child to use it as a symbol to 'mean' all drinks (for example) rather than the particular drink depicted. It is also the case that, contrary to normal development, children with ASDs will often find it easier to learn to read and use a written script (usually computer-generated) than to speak, and many children with ASDs have learnt to speak through first learning to read. Nor does the use of one system preclude the use of another, and many children's needs are best met through a combination of systems.

The precursors column does not mean that staff and parents have to wait until these precursors have been met before working with a system. They are there to show what the child needs to learn first in order to use the system, but the child will develop the precursors often through actual practice in communicating need. In the objects of reference system, it is necessary, for example, for the child to associate a toilet roll with going to the toilet, but the child learns to do this by being given a toilet roll and being taught to use it to signal that s/he is going to the toilet. At the start this is just a mechanical association but, by building it into a routine, and then gradually allowing the child to do more and more of the work in picking up the toilet roll, the 'meaning' is made apparent to the child as well as to others.

Something to communicate *for*

Even when a child can speak or has an alternative system of communication, that does not guarantee communication, especially in ASDs. Children also have to have a reason to communicate. That means they must not be able to do everything for themselves, nor have every need anticipated. This sometimes can happen in ASDs where children may be very adept at climbing to find whatever is needed, and parents may initially have encouraged this as a sign of independence. It may also be that the child controls the routines in a family, because s/he makes such a fuss if things are not exactly as s/he wants them. Parents are 'punished' (by the child having a tantrum) if the needs are not anticipated, and so they learn to always have things just as the child likes them. It is very easy to see how such patterns develop, but the child then has no reason to communicate and if there is little understanding, communication will not develop. Parents and staff may have to engineer (or even sabotage) things so that the child does have a clear need to communicate.

At school this problem arises in that staff often think they are teaching communication when in fact they are teaching the child to conform and be polite. There is nothing wrong with that, but the child will still need to be taught to communicate, and it is best if that is done first, in order not to further confuse the child. A typical situation is drinks time, where the children are seated and drinks and other goodies may be placed in front of them (well within reach), but the children are prevented from helping themselves until they have 'asked' for the item in some acceptable way (passed across a symbol, said the word, signed 'please' or whatever). This is fine for children who already understand what communication is, but not for the child with an ASD. What is needed is for the children to have to ask, because the desired object cannot be got without help or because there is a choice and the adult needs to know which one has been chosen. Under those conditions, waiting for the child's response is appropriate, as long as the child has been taught (and understands how to use) a way of communicating.

Children with ASDs may also communicate in bizarre or at least unusual ways and parents and staff may not recognise them as forms of communication. This means that the children's basic attempts at communication are often overlooked and, especially with the understanding of communication being so fragile, children may give up on these attempts, resorting to earlier forms of expressing feelings through challenging behaviour.

Thus, an important part of communication training is helping a child with an ASD understand why as well as how to communicate. Children will need to learn to see others as sources of having their needs met, and staff and parents will need to be helped to see how the child is communicating (at whatever level) and make the most of it.

Communicative functions

Long before babies can speak, they have already learnt to communicate many things: to let others know what they want, protest, express frustration, point things out to other people, make others laugh, 'show off', express anger, to be coy and above all to share in the emotions of those around them. While still having only a few words, toddlers will have begun to 'tease' others, to play games like 'peek-a-boo!' and to communicate in pretend games indicating that they know the teapot is empty as they pretend to pour a cup. The young child can also understand all these functions as others express them. It is only when we look at the development of a young child with an ASD that we see only a very few communicative functions developing, whether or not the child is speaking.

Children with ASDs, if they communicate at all, do so, unless specifically taught, with two (or at the most three) functions only. These are request (for something, or for someone to do something), protest and, for those with speech, 'lecturing' about a favourite topic. The latter is more like 'lecturing' than talking, since the child does not pause for others to have a turn and shows very little awareness of how the audience is reacting to the 'lecture'. Of course the child also expresses emotions, especially frustration, anger and fear, but this expression is like a very direct act, without any communicative intent. The child will scream with rage whether or not someone is there to hear and there is little effect from the actions of others, whether this is offering comfort or being angry or even laughing.

These first few basic communicative functions, to get needs met, are all that seem to develop spontaneously in ASDs, whether the child is speaking or being taught an alternative such as symbol or sign. Parents and staff may teach polite communicative functions (to greet people, to say goodbye when they leave, to thank people when they give you things, and so on), but children with ASDs only seem to acquire them as learnt habits, used only when they are cued, e.g. 'What do you say?' when handed a biscuit, 'Wave bye-bye' as granny is leaving.

The first thing to do, therefore, is to note the different communicative functions used by a child, and the form they take (speech, sign, picture, symbol, object) – see Table 6.2. Context should be recorded because some children may only use some functions with some people or in some situations (requests with parents, perhaps, comment at school where it has been taught). If the child has no communicative functions, then it is probably best to start with request since that is the easiest to illustrate and teach, and children with ASDs usually acquire this first. After that, protest is useful, giving the child an opportunity to express choice, and then there are a range of options. One of the most difficult is teaching a child with an ASD to comment – to point things out to other people just for the sake of doing so, and not because the item is wanted. It is valuable to teach because, once it has been mastered, it enables the child to learn any new vocabulary item, and not be limited to things s/he would want to ask for.

Function	Form (speech/sign/ symbol/object/ manipulates)	Context (with whom, where, when)	*Spontaneous/ prompted/ absent
Requests object (e.g. toy/food/ drink)			
Requests social routine/action (e.g. to be tickled)			
Requests help			
Requests more			
Protests/rejects			
Comments			
Denies			
Informs			
Greets			
Seeks information			
Deceives			

Table 6.2 Checklist for early communicative functions

* Three observations of spontaneous performance to count

Starting communication with a 'non-communicative' child

Where there appears to be little or no communication, then it is important to teach the child, as early as possible, how to influence others to get something, rather than just trying to use them physically, and to understand the communication of others. This can be done using a number of different systems, but here are two illustrations: one involves a child with poor understanding of pictures or symbols and the other involves using a systematic symbol programme, the PECS programme, to teach basic understanding of how to communicate.

1. Using objects of reference

Tom was a little boy of three years of age with autism and severe learning difficulties. He appeared to have very little, if any, communicative functions and he strongly resisted interruption or change in his 'routine' occupations of spinning and twiddling. He also had a visual problem, having a limited visual field, and did not seem to understand speech at all. It was a priority for Tom, therefore, that he learn a way of communicating his needs and that staff and parents also had a way of communicating to him what was going to happen. It was decided to start with objects of reference for him, given their tactile properties and the clear way he could be enabled to attend to them (through handling). Since toileting was a big issue with his mother at home, and was a social barrier in the nursery he attended, this was tackled first.

- The communication started by giving him a toilet roll to hold as a signal that he was being taken to the toilet. It took a month of consistent use at home and school before he accepted the toilet roll to 'mean' 'we are going to the toilet' and stopped his former angry resistance at being led away.

- Once he seemed to recognise the toilet roll as a signal for the toilet, the staff at his nursery started to prompt him to pick up the roll himself and give it to a member of staff to indicate where he was going.

- Eventually, he was taught to locate the roll himself and give it to an appropriate person before going to the toilet.

- Once established at school, this latter programme was transferred to the home.

- Other items were then added in similar ways, e.g. a cup to mean 'drink', a spoon to mean 'food'.

2. Using PECS

Although there has been a lot of work in introducing PECS into school and pre-school settings, home still remains the best place to start a PECS programme, if at all possible, because it is in that context that the child's desires can best be anticipated. This is important because otherwise one has to get into the artificial situation of teaching a child to ask for something s/he is offered, which is quite a strange thing to do. Since children with autism do not understand the natural communicative rules, it is not a good idea to introduce them to yet more unnatural ones.

Mary was a five year-old child with autism, a little speech (mostly echoed) and the only way of communicating being to drag people to what she wanted and 'throw' their hands in the desired direction. The priority was to get Mary to start using a system of communication spontaneously and further to accept when she could not have everything she asked for (or she would be a tyrant at home). Mary had a habit of watching *Thomas the Tank Engine* videos every afternoon when she returned from nursery and this was tackled first since it was already a source of family strife, as brothers and sisters protested at having to watch them constantly.

- The first afternoon of the programme, Mary came home from nursery to find no *Thomas* in the video, but instead a large Velcro sheet by the door on which was attached the empty video box of the *Thomas the Tank Engine* video. Mum was standing by this, not looking at it or her but with a flat hand outstretched just beneath the video box.

- Dad had brought Mary back from the nursery and before she could have a temper tantrum because *Thomas* was not there, he (without saying a word) prompted her to take the box off the Velcro board and place it in mother's outstretched hand.

- As soon as the box touched her hand, Mum sprang to life, said 'Oh! you want your *Thomas* video' and immediately put it on for her as usual. Mary was bemused, but had her tape and so was not disturbed.

- This scenario was repeated daily with Dad gradually hanging back from prompting her until Mary was coming in, getting the box by herself and placing it in her mother's hand.

- From this point Mum started to move away from the board and then to move her hand down until eventually Mary had to follow her around with the video box to make the exchange. At this point she was taught to make a sound (Mum) to get attention, before handing over the box. Another child without any speech might be taught to tap the adult on the arm.

- This indicated that Mary 'had the idea' of exchanging the box for the video and attracting an adult's attention to do it. The next step in this case was to make the video box more like a usual PECS symbol (a picture rather than a box and reduced in size) and then begin to introduce other symbols for other things (or events, such as ten minutes on the swing) at other times.

- This was the time to introduce that other advantage of the PECS programme: the notion of a menu. The symbols from which Mary could choose were always on a board. It was decided to tackle the issue of Mary always having the same *Thomas* video as she came home each day, by not including that video in the symbols to choose from on the board. Mary had also been used to following visual schedules (from the TEACCH programme) at nursery and at home (for dressing in the mornings). Thus, to make this transition easier for her, she was also shown a visual schedule which displayed the current board (with its menu of choices) and the 'next menu' (on which *Thomas* did appear). It was judged that Mary would not have coped with not having *Thomas* available on the menu without the security of the schedule 'telling' her that it would be available after this one.

- Mary was able to follow the schedule, making a choice from the current menu and then choosing *Thomas* when the next menu presented itself.

PECS continues with teaching sentence structures of 'I want X' and then other communicative functions such as comment, 'I see X', but it is the first basic ideas that are its real strength and, once mastered, early years staff may develop their own ways of building on the child's understanding (with the help of an SLT), although the routines and structures of PECS make it attractive for children with ASDs (and staff).

Sounds have meaning

Although stressing communication as of prime importance, speech sounds should not be neglected. However, it is not a good idea to teach the child to say sounds and words without meaning, because that is just teaching them to be echolalic. There is no harm in encouraging the child to vocalise to accompany communicative attempts as they exchange objects or pictures or words, but vocalisation as such is often most successful when supported by the structure of music and rhythm. Get into the habit of providing a little sung commentary to the child's actions:

Danny, Danny is washing his hands, washing his hands, washing his hands
Danny, Danny is washing his hands and the soap goes round and round
Danny's made a lather, a lather, a lather, Danny's made a lather
And now he rinses it off

You can choose whatever tune you can get to fit, and you can vary the words but try to keep the essential elements of the song, repetition and an easy-to-remember tune that emphasises key words, matching them to actions. Singing also helps you to slow down your speech and the child is more able to understand what the words mean. Once the child is very familiar with this sung routine, introduce opportunities for the child to complete a rhythm sequence with the appropriate sung word, by leaving a very exaggerated pause with a lead-in emphasising the gap, thus:

Danny, Danny is washing his hands, washing his hands, washing his hands
Danny, Danny is washing his hands and the soap goes round and ...

After an uncomfortably long time, if the child does not respond, just complete it yourself and carry on. Nearly always, the child will eventually supply the missing word (even if it is not very clear) and once again just continue. If you stop excitedly to make a fuss and praise the child you may 'throw' him/her and make it harder to do it next time.

If you want to practise particular speech sounds (with the advice of an SLT), then also do so in a rhythmic game of imitation and make it fun, clearly marking it as a game and not related to communication training which is also being taught.

Understanding instructions

Singing instructions often feels strange, but can be a good way of getting the child to understand and, if the action wanted is emphasised by the tune, to obey. The tune that leads into the instruction helps the children prepare to obey, and children with ASDs are far more likely to obey if they have time to get used to the idea, rather than expecting them to change direction suddenly (e.g. to sit down when they are running around). It does not have to be long or elaborate but just 'singing' *All the children should now sit DOWN* is often better than just saying, 'Children, sit down!'

It is important to give instructions confidently and to say exactly what you mean – think dog training – in that the key instruction should be emphasised and there should be no polite idioms that might make the child think there is a choice, when there is not. Thus say, 'Robin, here, now, reading time' rather than 'Would you like to come and sit next to me, Robin dear, it's time to read.' Children with ASDs need direct instructions, not wrapped up as questions or statements, or offering them opportunities to refuse. A good tip is to offer a choice of two things, especially when you suspect the child does not want to do either. You should not say, 'Will you write your name for me now, James?' but rather, 'James, are you going to write your name with the red or the blue pen?' This is more effective if James is really into colours, thus distracting him from the writing task itself into something he is interested in.

The other key aspect to instruction is that it is far more likely to be understood and obeyed if it is visual rather than oral. The visual cue should be one that 'fits' the task, wherever possible. Thus, if you want the children to sit on their chairs, rather than putting their name or photo on the chair (although you can have this as well, as a teaching aid) draw round the child's seated bottom and then stick on a pink (or brown) shape to match that bottom. The child with an ASD is then usually happy to 'match' his/her bottom to the right chair. In the same way, drawing round objects onto paper that lines surfaces, enables the children to replace items happily in the right place when asked to tidy away. Children can learn to do the right things in the right area, if they are clearly marked out as the 'floor play area', 'the book area' and so on. Conversely, you can expect trouble if you bring a child to the table where they normally have drinks time and expect the child to work – the table will be 'telling' the child that this is time for drinks. If you must use the same table for multiple purposes, then make each purpose distinct by, for example, covering it with a different coloured cloth.

Having a visual timetable (of two activities just to start with, then three and so on) will help the child understand the TEACCH principle of 'work then play' and so will enable you to extend the range of tasks the child will attempt. Having a daily timetable (once the child has understood the principle and worked up from shorter ones) will enable the child to understand what has to happen before mummy comes, or before playtime, or whatever. It is very hard for children with ASDs to learn to wait without this visual way of marking the time passing. When getting the child to work alone, set up a little distraction-free corner and teach the child to find the task to do on his/her left, to do it, and then to place the finished task to the right. This is made easier if there are baskets for the tasks to do and baskets for the finished work. Alternatively, the child can be taught to work to a colour matching system with a work schedule left to right with different coloured stickers. The child takes each sticker in turn and finds the task it belongs to, matches it, brings it back to the work station to do, and then moves on to the next sticker in line as that task is finished. The 'task' need not be an academic one, but something like getting dressed. Just giving the child the pile of clothes often results in the child getting in a muddle and being frustrated, whereas matching each item in turn to a visual schedule, before putting that item on, makes the task easier for the child and more attractive as well.

Chapter Seven

Developing social understanding and enabling play

The social problem in ASDs

Not all children with ASDs are socially aloof and withdrawn. Sometimes children with ASDs can be really anxious to play with others but they do not seem to get it right, often being too boisterous or trying to do everything in their own way. What is common to all those with an ASD is that they are not able to process social and emotional information easily and naturally as others do. They have instead to try to work out what they or others are thinking or feeling. This means that they take a long time to process social and emotional information. Just slowing down and giving them longer to respond can make a big difference to their responsiveness. It also means that they cannot process this information while they are trying to do something else, so they find it very difficult to learn to do something new while in a social group. If they have to learn something new, this is best one-to-one with a familiar adult, or taught in a non-social way by organising it for them through visual instruction or through a computer. Conversely, if you want them to respond well to others, it is best having a task with which the children with ASDs are already familiar. This will enable them to concentrate on the reactions of others.

There will be a range of reactions to other children among those with ASDs. Some will just be able to ignore them, not focusing on them at all unless they are actually interfered with. Others will be in constant fear, not knowing what the other children are likely to do next and finding their noise and running around unpredictable and terrifying. It is important for children with ASDs that they do learn to tolerate others and even to engage with them. This will open up so many more learning opportunities in the future and make their lives more comfortable, with far fewer sources of anxiety. If we can help young children with ASDs to understand others and even to enjoy being with them, we can enable them to enter a more 'normal' developmental route and prevent most of the secondary consequences of ASDs.

First impressions

Imagine having to go to work in a country whose language and customs you do not understand. The first morning you arrive you are faced with a large room with people rushing around everywhere, talking loudly and quickly to one another, with lots of flashing signs and public announcements in a language you do not understand. Depending on your personality, you might run away and never come back, retreat into a corner, cover your ears and look on in dismay, trying to puzzle out where to go and what to do, or you might stop someone forcefully and demand attention and someone to show you the ropes. This situation is not unlike that which often faces young children with ASDs entering a busy early years environment. Like the hypothetical you, it depends on their personality whether they run away, withdraw and try anxiously to work things out or whether they forcefully make their presence felt to adults or other children.

What you (and they) need in such a situation is a clear guide in a language you understand. You need to be shown to a quiet place where announcements and signs are minimal and where you are clearly shown what to do, for how long, what next and so on. In time, you will want to learn the customs and language of the country you are working in. However, the first step is to reduce anxiety and stress, make the task manageable, and gradually introduce those language and cultural lessons. For the child, this means that there should be a clear visual signal when s/he enters that shows him/her where to go, what to do when s/he gets there, when it is finished, what to do next and so on. The work place for the child should also provide a shield against a lot of the noise and bustle of the early years environment. In particular the child should be seated so that others are not approaching him/her from behind or running around his/her back – both situations that make the child with an ASD very anxious and disturbed.

The system of visual instruction can be taken from the TEACCH programme and be objects (arranged in shelves to give the order of tasks top to bottom or left to right, or hung up on pegs, as appropriate), pictures or symbols. The child should be guided to take the first symbol, picture or object and match it to one placed in the appropriate place. Many early years environments start the day with a greeting and social group session. But there is often a lot of toing and froing as children arrive at slightly different times, so it is best to have the children take something quiet to do in their own corner to begin with. Then have the social group a bit later, when everyone has arrived. Most children with ASDs should be able to manage a group session if it is structured for them, but a new child may not be able to do so at once. It is a bad idea to force a child to participate since they learn to be disruptive and to waste energy on resisting. It is far better that a very brief period is planned and carried out successfully, since that can be extended. Entry to a social group session for a new highly distractible child, then, might take the following steps:

- Before the session starts make a plastic or strong paper cutout of the child's bottom and let the child practise sitting on it in the environment in which the child will have to sit. This may be a chair in a circle (with a large space either side to prevent interference with or from other children) or a mat on the floor.

- When the social group time commences, position the child with you a long way from the group. Clearly indicate a visual schedule (perhaps on a clipboard) that gives the structure of the session so that parts can be turned over as they occur. An example structure would be: singing greeting song; calling register; doing the date chart; teacher talking; teacher asks questions and children talking one by one; visual timetable for the morning; 'time to work' song. The child will not understand the structure at first, but can come to do so through repetition and practice.

- If the child is restless at any point, quickly insert a personal instruction such as 'Jamie goes to work now' symbol so that you in effect give Jamie permission to leave. If this staying for only a few minutes lasts more than ten days, however, it is time to rethink. In that case just bring him to his seat a few minutes before the end of the session so that now he leaves as the others do. Then work back from there, giving him longer each time, but always leaving with the others.

- Persist with taking the child each day, even if it takes a long time for him/her to manage more than a few minutes. Eventually, the child will be sitting throughout the session, albeit apart from it. At this point begin slowly approaching the group, inch by inch, until the child is sitting alongside (but not too close) to the others.

- Always be alert to insert the personal permission symbol, if the child becomes restless. It is important that the child does not develop a habit of running off and being chased or that will become a far more interesting activity than joining the group and will be far more difficult to remedy.

Making a relationship with an adult

The child will have problems making all relationships, but will find it easier to do so with adults than with other children. The adult chosen should be a key worker (or parent) since this is the person who can reinforce the strategies for communication and joint attention in daily activities with the child. However, although the bulk of the work will be done during these daily activities, it is important to set aside some time each day (at least 20 minutes, preferably an hour) for a special one-to-one time in which to establish early turn-taking and reciprocal interaction games. A quiet distraction-free environment is required with some comfortable seating, floor space and a few stimulus objects, such as chiffon scarves, a drum, a bubble kit and so on. There should be something to share interest with the adult, but not enough to make the objects more interesting than the person.

The format of the interaction should be as described in Chapter Four, basically mirroring, but slowing down and exaggerating the early interactive routines of a baby and its mother. The adult must learn to wait far longer than expected for the child's response and then emphasise and feed it back to the child. A good guide to hold in your head is, 'Is s/he enjoying this?' The child's way of showing enjoyment may be unusual so you must be sensitive to this. Once you are 'tuned in' to how the child expresses pleasure then find an interaction that the child enjoys and try to extend it, always being ready to retreat back if the answer to the question becomes 'no'. Remember that singing can help the child see structure in social interactions that otherwise s/he might be blind to. This is a good opportunity to encourage appropriate vocal games and filling in words in songs. Boisterous children may need to start with vigorous chasing, tickling and rough and tumble games and gradually come to quieter play (perhaps using music to alter the mood). Children who are more touch sensitive may prefer to start very gently, with imitation from afar, gradually encroaching on the child's space, but always remembering to ask the question and retreat to an earlier position if the answer is 'no'. It is better to have a successful long distance relationship with a child than to force things too quickly so that the aversiveness of being near others is reinforced.

Remember also to be sensitive to parents. You cannot expect a parent to be unequivocally overjoyed when told that a member of staff has a close personal relationship with their child, the same child who struggles away from their embraces, does not go to them to be comforted and seems to treat them as mere objects. That is why it is often best to use parents as this first adult. This may not be possible for practical reasons or simply because parents are so upset by their child's lack of responsiveness that they cannot stop themselves forcing the issue and frightening the child away. However, always approach the task with the parents' understanding that you are going to work out how to do it, and then pass on your techniques to them. This is obviously to everyone's benefit and the child, having done it once with you, will actually be more receptive. Also you can video your sessions and use them to train parents step-by-step and then get parents to video themselves for you to go through with them (if needed). Often it is enough for them to see it themselves to see what they are doing 'wrong' – jumping in too soon, perhaps, giving the child conflicting or multiple instructions and so on.

Enabling relationships with other children

It is very hard for a child with an ASD to relate to people, so it is best to start that skill with an adult who can make all the adjustments necessary and do most of the 'work' in the relationship. However, even after learning to relate to adults, the child with an ASD is going to find it very difficult to relate to an untrained adult, let alone a child. That is why it is important to give them the skills to play as other children do, so that there is a focus for the interaction, which can then happen more naturally around this play. There has been extensive work in the United States, Canada and Europe showing that young children can benefit enormously from play interaction with typically developing peers, but that this needs to be structured (Wolfberg, 1999). Just putting the children together in the hope that the child with the ASD will 'pick up' the necessary social skills nearly always ends in failure. Equally, giving them an untrained 'minder' only rarely works (and then it is because of the exceptional personal qualities and commitment of these members of staff). Without knowing how to guide the interaction, the adult just becomes another barrier to its occurring.

It used to be thought that the answer was to train the normally developing children to be play partners to the children with ASDs. But then it was found that the children with ASDs could only play with these trained children and not with others. Roeyers (1996) found that it was a better strategy to just give the other children some ideas of the difficulties the children with ASDs were having in playing and to reassure them that staff would be there to support them. This was more efficient in getting the children to devise their own way of engaging the children. The children with ASDs who learnt to play with the children in this way, were also more able to play with other children and so had presumably been taught to recognise play signals that were more natural than the ones adults had 'taught' the children to use.

It can take a while to teach children with ASDs to play in ways that their peers will not find boring or bizarre. While this is being worked on, therefore, it is a good idea to capitalise on the few social games children with ASDs do often enjoy. A clear favourite is chasing. Other children need to recognise that when the little boy with an ASD is pushing them and running away he does not mean to be horrid. He just wants to play chasing and does not understand how to tell them this. This can stop some of their fear of the child and they can then be involved in deciding what to teach him as a signal to play chase and how to organise that. The danger in ASDs, however, is that once the boy finds something he enjoys, he will want to do it all the time. If the signal to play does not come often enough, he may well go back to pushing or hitting. Thus, we should keep to clear signals for the start and end of chasing times (backed up with a visual schedule that says when the next session is coming and what has to happen in between) which are rigidly enforced. The other children may need to be monitored for illicit little chasing games, which may be fun and part of normal child naughtiness, but will ruin the programme for the child with the ASD, if left unchecked.

To help with the management of this, it is a good idea to have lots of chasing games when first introduced (they can be quite short sessions), but to work on reducing them and building up other social games. Structured musical games are a good idea because the music will help the child with the ASD to participate and the imitation and joint action routines are valuable learning experiences. Turn-taking games (often mediated by music) are also valuable and fun for most children. Games like 'Petronella', where a child takes turns to be in the middle of the circle, to perform an action for the others to copy, involve a lot of valuable social learning. Once again the song and repetition involved also helps the child with the ASD anticipate and then participate. You may need to be lax about the rule that the action chosen should be different each time, because that will be a step too far for most young children with ASDs.

Games like musical bumps (where children have to sit when the music stops) are valuable in helping the child time his/her actions, co-ordinate actions with those of the group and learn to sit on command. This latter is a very useful skill when it comes to managing difficult behaviour. Just learning to walk round to music helps the child with an ASD to match steps with others and to gain valuable experience in walking alongside others. This is an extremely important skill to acquire in the early years to avoid years of being told off for hanging back or running ahead, without having had the experience of walking to another's pace.

For the slightly older child, who has already mastered these musical social games, there is a good party game which helps teach them about how people know things and that someone can know something and another person cannot. This is very hard for children with ASDs to understand and normally developing children still struggle with aspects of it until around four years old. This 'concrete' and motivating version, however, is usually successful at giving them some understanding.

Sweet game

- You need a selection of attractive sweets of very distinctive appearance, a plate and some bags with names on for the children. Play it as a small circle game or the children become fed up waiting for their turn.

- A small number of sweets – say five, all different from one another – are placed on a plate and a child whose turn it is is sent away so s/he cannot see.

- The other children then choose one sweet to be 'IT'. The children are reminded that the child outside does not know what sweet is IT because s/he was not there when it was chosen.

- They must not tell him/her but only say 'yes' or 'no' when the child holds up each sweet in turn.

- The child comes back, chooses a sweet to hold up and asks, 'Is this IT?'

- If the answer is 'No!', the sweet goes in a bag for the child to keep and another sweet is held up.

- This continues until the IT sweet is chosen when the choosing stops and it is the next child's turn.

Thus everyone gets at least one sweet and the lucky ones may get all five. Any game involving inequality of outcome is hard for young children to accept, but it is also a valuable lesson in life, especially for the children with ASDs. They often have a poor sense of personal possession and have to have lots of opportunities to reinforce the need to respect ownership, even if someone does have something you want and have not got. The very clear explicit rules help make this acceptable in the context of this game.

Teaching advanced cognitive play

Play level	Example	Elicited	Spontaneous
1. Sensori-motor – simple	Toys related to perceptual properties of toy with only one 'use' per item, e.g. smell, taste, spinning		
2. Sensori-motor – combinational	Relating two or more items together in same way each time, e.g. stacks bricks, uses posting box		
3. Sensori-motor – exploratory	Relates to toys (single or combinational) in more than one way, e.g. spins as well as stacks blocks		
4. Functional play	Treats toy as toy function (not symbolic – understood at toy level only) e.g. puts doll to bed, operates train on track		
5. Symbolic play a) object substitution	Pretends one object is another, e.g. a stick becomes a train		
b) pretend qualities	Pretends a quality, e.g. that a toy cooker is hot		
c) pretend existence	Pretends something exists that does not, e.g pours 'tea' from an empty teapot		
d) narrative sequences	Plays (acts out) a sequence of imaginary events that 'tell a story'		

Table 7.1 Levels of cognitive play skills

Children with ASDs often have very limited play patterns and rarely play with other children. The two facts are not unconnected in that it is hard for children with ASDs to play with others if they do not share common play interests and skills. Conversely, it is playing with others that helps children develop their play and not become stuck in inflexible routines and habits.

In some ways, teaching play can seem odd, because play is something we do naturally, to relax, and if it has to be taught it feels more like work. However, we cannot just assume that the child with an ASD is *choosing* to play with a toy car, for example, just by spinning its wheels, if that child is not aware of other possibilities for play with a toy car and does not have the skills to exploit those possibilities. Thus, it is part of education to ensure that a child is enabled to take advantage of all these possibilities in play and only if s/he reverts to spinning after that, can we say that is an informed play choice. Table 7.1 gives a hierarchy of play skills (related to cognitive complexity, not social play development) as a chart for assessing the child's level of skill.

Once assessed, the child should be given training in the next stage and many opportunities to practise those play skills, once acquired, before moving on to the next. Elicited play is where the adult provides a model for the child to copy or instructs the child to play in a particular way. Spontaneous play is where this play is engaged in by the child, unprompted, on three different occasions. Beyer and Gammeltoft (2000) give a very useful framework for observing children with ASDs at play, as do Cumine et al, (2000), and Sherratt and Peter (2002) give schedules for developing play levels and lots of ideas on how to engage children with ASDs at the different levels. They also show how to take the play further into the development of full narrative sequences and socio-drama. They give many ideas that will be useful to enrich the play of children with ASDs in the early years, although they are not aiming particularly at this age group and some of the developments will be for later years. Nevertheless, it is very useful to start the processes in the early years and to understand the framework in which these skills are being developed.

In engaging the child at each stage the principles of working with these children remain the same. These can be summarised as:

- Start at the child's level, observe and mirror the child's actions (imitate in a way that draws the imitation to the child's attention, e.g. sit next to the child facing a mirror – a child will be more able to focus on a reflected image than to make direct eye contact).

- Once the imitation has been attended to, set up a sequence of turn-taking between you and the child.

- Once the turn-taking is established, introduce a variation in the imitation and try to elicit the child's imitation of you.

- Once the child is imitating you regularly, try to develop the child's play to the next level, e.g. introducing new ways of playing with a toy (for a child at level 1) or ways of combining toys in play.

- Remember the importance of having fun in the interaction and involving the child emotionally.

Chapter Eight

Managing behaviour

Behaviour problems and ASDs

For many early years staff the biggest problem in working with children with ASDs is managing what appears to be very unpredictable and often severe behavioural tantrums. There will be many children in early years settings who have not yet understood all the social rules and do not have the behavioural control to conform. Given that many young children with ASDs will also have general learning difficulties, it is to be expected that much of their behaviour and reactions will be immature and need training. However, there are particular problems associated with children with ASDs and staff will need to develop particular ways of understanding and dealing with their behaviour.

As explored earlier, it is necessary to understand the behaviour if it is to be managed effectively. Effective methods of management depend on skills in developing alternative behaviours (such as communication) and setting up 'autism-friendly' environments. It is useful first, however, to understand why difficult and challenging behaviour is associated with ASDs so that it becomes possible to see the behaviour in a developmental light. On a bad day it can seem as if the child is 'deliberately' targeting you or even vulnerable children, but this is almost never the case, at least in its normal sense. The behaviour arises directly from the children's difficulties and it is their reaction to the difficult confusing world in which they find themselves. If behaviour is mismanaged, then it may be that the child learns to behave in difficult ways or does things to get particular responses. But it is understanding the meaning of that behaviour that will help us prevent or change that behaviour.

Particular problems in ASDs

Immaturity

Many behavioural patterns in ASDs are the result of immaturity, in particular of the systems for monitoring and control of their own behaviour and emotions. Even for the most able, their attentional and emotional control may be below the level of a nine-month-old and so the behaviour shown is at a similar level. If the children are acting out their anger or fear directly, without any conscious awareness, then they have little chance of controlling that behaviour without external help. Children with ASDs will find it almost impossible to control their impulses (no matter what the 'punishment') unless they are trained to perform another response to the same stimulus.

Helpful strategies to try

Even though the problem may stem from immature systems, that does not mean one just has to 'wait' for development. Most children with ASDs will benefit from some of the strategies suggested in earlier chapters for helping them understand their own emotions in real situations.

There are also practical ways of controlling impulsive behaviour on a daily basis. Rather than telling children with ASDs not to do something or to stop doing something, you should train them to do something else in response to that situation. Thus you do not say, 'Don't kick the back of Mandy's chair, Tom!' For a start, Tom's name should start the command so that he can learn to pay attention to the command and realise it is directed to him. Then, you are telling him what *not* to do without saying what *should* be done and the child with an ASD will find it very difficult to decide on an action, given a 'free' choice. In addition this instruction directs his attention to the behaviour you do not want, i.e. the kicking. What you need to say is something like, 'Tom (pause to wait for attention), put your feet on the marks on the floor' where Tom's chair is at the right height for this to happen and where 'feet shaped' marks (from plastic) have been placed on the floor and Tom trained previously to use them. Similar visual controls in the environment (such as 'stop' signs hung over light switches or put next to doors – to be turned to 'go' when it is time to go through the door) can reduce a lot of disruptive behaviour.

The strategy outlined above will work if Tom is just kicking as an absent-minded habit, but what if he is kicking in a rage? In that case, we need to think more about what has caused the rage, and try to intervene earlier, before Tom's behaviour has got out of his (and often our) control. Even then, a familiar strategy of putting his feet on the mark (or sitting down to the command 'sit', which has been well trained) can work in helping to calm him down and giving staff time to think of other strategies and distractions to try. You need to observe children carefully and note the signs of them getting 'worked up', which nearly always precede a behavioural outburst. Once you can recognise such signs (perhaps the child gets hot and restless and may begin to fidget or flap his hands or may start to jump), then that is the point to come in with an alternative distracting behaviour. You also need to record what has led up to the anger so that a behaviour management plan can be put into operation. After the incident, staff need to consider what led up to the episode (or potential episode, if you managed to avert it) and to think what needs to be done. There are no single definitive answers, but the following questions help to focus staff on what you need to know:

- Does the child need further training to give him a skill he currently does not have?

- Does the classroom or lesson plan need to be changed to help the child avoid distressing or fearful situations?

- Is this a pattern of behaviour shown in other situations (including home) or is it limited to this one situation, and what can we learn from that?

- Were there any particular triggers for the behaviour? Look particularly at the level of staff language.

- Was this a 'last straw' phenomenon after a build-up of stress? What stressful events is the child being exposed to regularly?

Poor social awareness

Children with ASDs will have little or no understanding of what other people are likely to do or why or how others are reacting to their behaviour. They will, therefore, find others frightening and hard to predict and control. At the same time, they will be desperate to control them, in order to manage their own fear and uncertainty. They will have no natural ways of getting co-operation from children or adults and will be behaving in ways that others find bizarre or even offensive. They will have no intrinsic understanding of social rules and will not be responsive to the normal social sanctions that adults use to 'train' normally developing children in expected ways of behaving ('Big boys don't do that!' 'What will mummy say?' 'Would you like it if someone hit you like that?' 'Poor Jenny! You have hurt her. Say sorry!').

Helpful strategies to try

Children with ASDs do not understand about personal space. They will invade other people's regularly, without any understanding of how others will view them standing right under their nose or even interfering with their clothing, perhaps even stroking their legs. It is hard for them to differentiate how close to stand to people according to degree of familiarity and so it is best to give them a rather formal 'rule' about approaching others and to train them rigorously. A general useful social distance (although admittedly odd in a young child) is around 46cm (18 inches). Once this has been grasped, the children can be given very specific exceptions that will need training separately – parents and siblings perhaps, or maybe just parents if brothers and sisters need their space protecting.

A few children may not even be able to recognise their own parents, especially if they are out of context or are looking or smelling different in some way. They need a symbol that stands for 'mummy' and another that stands for 'daddy' and they need to be trained specifically in the concept of their mother and father. This has to be done tactfully as parents may be aware of something wrong, but can be devastated to find that their own child is not even recognising them as a person but relying on glasses, or perfume worn or some other object. Get lots of photographs (not just a single smiling shot – mum does not always look like that) of the parents looking in different directions, wearing different clothes, having different facial expressions and match them to these symbols. Also collect snatches of the parents talking on tape – again with very different vocal expressions – and match these to the symbols. Then get some video shots so that they match the symbols to their parents' moving images. Then use the symbols in greeting parents as they arrive and encourage their use when talking about parents at home and at school. They will also need to learn that the person they refer to as 'mummy' is the same as the one the staff call 'Mrs Talbot', and their daddy calls 'Margaret'. This kind of learning goes on in normal development, but there it happens naturally without detailed teaching, whereas it needs explicit instruction in ASDs.

When it comes to tolerating others coming near to them, the situation is very different. Many will have a sense of having their personal space invaded if someone comes within a few feet of them, especially if that person approaches without warning or comes from behind. It is just the kind of adaptation that you would make for children with sensory impairments. Deaf children need to be approached from a direction in which they can see you coming. Blind children need to be given auditory signals of your approach. Children with ASDs also need time to prepare for your coming and so you need to make sure they can see you coming and to approach slowly. It is wise at first to stop just at the border of the child's sense of personal space, just inside the area that the child starts to feel uncomfortable when it is invaded. Stay within that area until the child is comfortable with it. Then move a little nearer. It is a bit like the rules for interaction in Chapter Four. You are always trying to get the child to accept a little more intimacy, without overwhelming the child and forcing more withdrawal.

If you have to handle the child in any way, do warn them, but do not do it tentatively. Like children with cerebral palsy, it is far harder for them to tolerate weak tentative touches – leaving them confused about the boundaries of their own bodies and cut off from the world as they are overwhelmed with this unpleasant touch sensation. A firm grip is easier to manage, and usually more suited to your purpose.

All this complexity in approaching children with ASDs means that, like other forms of social interaction, it is best done first by adults. Once the child is comfortable at being approached by a number of adults, then other children can be encouraged to follow similar rules in approaching them. If the child with the ASD is used to playing with the other children in a game they all enjoy (such as chase), then they will often accept this stage without problems, but you need to be careful because they may try to change all interactions into chase games and get increasingly rough if their attempts to do this are rebuffed. Ideas for other social games (Chapter Seven and Barratt et al., 2000) should help with this.

Poor communication skills

If you do not understand how to communicate, or even what communication is, no matter whether or not you can speak, it is very difficult to influence others. This goes beyond not knowing how to ask for things or tell others what is wrong. It is about not 'reading' the communication of body, gesture, facial expression and tone of voice, and so not being able to understand the effect one is having on others or what they intend. People hardly ever say exactly what they mean and so, even if spoken words are understood, the child will often get an incomplete message or even a completely wrong message. The children's own attempts at communication may also be misunderstood or missed and so the children may learn progressively more extreme ways of trying to get their needs met.

Helpful strategies to try

It is often very helpful to treat a child's difficult behaviour as if it were an attempt at communication. Ask yourself, what would the child be telling me if they knew how to communicate? Sometimes, staff find this uncomfortable because they feel the answer is 'I don't want to do this' or 'Go away!' and that is against their teaching objective for the child. Should they not be teaching the child to conform and to learn that they cannot get away with things by biting others, or whatever? It is true that you should not be rewarding a child for biting or other challenging behaviour, which is why it is important for you to get in with your strategy before the difficult behaviour emerges. In respect to the worries about the curriculum, however, you have to think about priorities. Ask yourself the question, 'Is it more important that this boy learns to do this (whatever this is) now or that he learns another more acceptable way of telling me that he does not want to do it?' In nearly all cases, the answer is obviously that the communication skill is more important. You are not giving up on the first task; you are just giving it lower priority until the child has learnt a calm strategy of controlling his/her environment, when you can reintroduce it in a negotiated way.

Let us take an example of a boy who does not want to write his name over a dotted guide and reacts by screeching, sweeping the task onto the floor and biting whoever is at hand. You have observed this carefully and note that the trigger for the behaviour is being presented with this task. In your 'as if' analysis, you have decided that he needs another way of telling you he does not want to do it. However, you must start to teach this before he has screeched, swept it to the floor and bitten anyone, or these behaviours will just increase. Timing is thus crucial, but first you have to decide on the alternative behaviour to teach. Even though this boy has a few words, it is unlikely he will be able to think of them to use in this situation when he is expressing rage, rather than trying to communicate. You need to think of an alternative which is as easy for him as the difficult behaviour he is using and which will be easy for you to prompt. In this case, since he has been using a symbol system to ask for what he wants in other contexts, you choose a symbol that is to mean 'No' and you provide a familiar Velcro pad as a communication board on his table top, to which the symbol attaches.

After practising with another member of staff to get the timing right, you approach the child with the task in one hand and the symbol in the other. Then follow these steps:

- Present the task to the child and at the same time present the symbol by placing it next to the task on the table top.

- Before the child has a chance to react badly, physically prompt the child to pick up the symbol and place it on the communication board.

- As soon as it is placed on the board say, 'Oh, you say No; you don't want to do the writing' and at the same time remove the offending task.

- Leave the child for a noticeable time – say two minutes.

- Return with the task and the symbol and repeat the first four steps.

- Keep repeating this, but gradually do less and less of the prompting to pick up the symbol, until the child is using it by himself.

- Once this is happening calmly, then you can start negotiating with the boy about doing some of the task before removing it. In spite of the child's calmness, this should be done carefully or all the good work might be undone. Provide a TEACCH-type schedule that shows the task and then something else the child enjoys doing. Start off the task yourself and just leave the last bit for the child to do. Still let the child have the symbol with the task and when he displays it say, 'I know you want to say No; but first do just this little bit', indicating the task and the schedule.

- Next time do not give the 'No' symbol, but have it available to the child. Gradually increase the extent of the task until the child is accepting it all.

- Use the 'No' symbol in other situations to allow the child to reject something, where that is appropriate. It is important that the child retains the ability to protest and reject in an acceptable way, so you have to find ways of keeping this understanding going.

Sensory and medical problems

Although epilepsy may not show itself until later, there are sometimes associated disturbances of brain functioning which add to the children's difficulties in understanding and dealing with their world. Many of the children with ASDs, especially when young, will have problems in dealing with the sensory world, with fluctuating levels of sensitivity to noise, colour, light, skin sensitivity and pain awareness that reflect abnormal brain chemistry and reactivity. There is also some evidence that digestive problems may be particularly acute, with chronic constipation and associated gut problems causing behavioural disturbance at a number of different levels (Shattock et al., 2001). Many will have very poor levels of body awareness and react badly to unstructured space (often hugging the perimeter of large rooms or outdoor play spaces) or invasion of their personal space (which may be a very large area). It may make it difficult for them to tolerate some forms of clothing (especially shoes) or to sit on a seat for all but the briefest of periods.

Helpful strategies to try

You need to make whatever adjustments are possible to make the environment comfortable for the child and to enable the child to learn without stress. There may be some things which cannot be altered in which case you need to help the child gradually to become desensitised to them. Giving the child earphones to wear (perhaps with gentle music to listen to) can often help the child focus on an activity and not be disturbed by the natural noises of a busy early years environment. Allow the child to work in the carpeted classroom without shoes but insist on shoes for outside wear. Co-operate with parents to give the child loose clothing (tracksuits are often best) of soft material that do not continually disturb them.

Talk to parents about diet and be observant about possible situations where the child is uncomfortable or even in pain. Be aware that constipation often produces overflow, which may be mistaken for diarrhoea and treated in a way that adds to the child's problems. Make yourself knowledgeable about any diets the child is on and co-operate with parents in helping to monitor their effects. Gluten and caseine (the main protein in milk) free diets have been claimed to help with behaviour problems in ASDs, but it is important that such diets are done systematically under the control of a dietician to avoid dangerous deficiencies, especially where a child has a very restrictive diet. Have additive and caffeine-free drinks and snacks in the early years setting, as these substances are likely to add to any problems in hyperactivity that may exist. Introduce periods of relaxation with soft music, dim light and relaxing oils in the atmosphere to help the children calm down at the end of a busy period. Conversely, introduce a daily period of rigorous aerobic exercise (20 minutes a day) to reduce stress and to help regulate the child's sleep patterns.

Physical difficulties

Children with ASDs sometimes have additional physical difficulties or have extreme motor responsiveness to their environment. Thus, some have dyspraxic problems which mean they can do things automatically if they are not thinking about it (pick up a pencil, drink from a cup, climb a ladder), but they cannot plan and intend an action so they are unable to do these same tasks if instructed to do so. If this is not understood it looks as if the child is being wilful and could do the task if s/he wanted. Some children are ataxic (clumsy) and they may have very poor balance to the extent that they find it very difficult (and often become very fearful) when asked to walk on uneven surfaces such as sand, or even grass. Once more, this is often misunderstood as a behaviour problem. Other children are extremely agile and seem to have absolutely no sense of danger. They can become obsessed with something (chimney pots, walking down the white lines in the middle of the road) which can put them at great risk – and seem to get particular pleasure from being high above the ground and walking on narrow ledges. Nor do they understand any social inhibitions associated with climbing or investigation, and may climb up bookcases in libraries or shops, or enjoy the sensation of running and leaping (often accompanied by a loud shout) in a church. Any attempt to get them to come back can make it worse as it turns the climb into a chasing game.

Helpful strategies to try

For the child with significant dyspraxic or clumsy motor patterns, it is important to get the advice of a knowledgeable physiotherapist or occupational therapist. Such a person can give an assessment of the child's problems and some strategies for handling the difficulties and exercises to help the child's physical development. Management strategies may include making sure the child's feet are anchored when sitting so the child does not have to use arms to balance and can then concentrate on tasks such as writing. Exercises might involve posture exercises and learning to cross the body midline with arms and to walk and crawl so that arms and legs move in a co-ordinated way. As with so much else, movement to music can be a valuable way of building these basic skill patterns.

For the child with a dangerous habit of climbing or running in the road, more behavioural strategies are needed. Try to give the child some exciting adventure experiences, but in a controlled environment. Then clearly differentiate times and places when such climbing or running is allowed, from situations when it is not. In the forbidden areas or at the forbidden times, remember that it is not effective just to forbid an action, but to concentrate on what the child should be doing instead. Train the child to follow the line of the kerb on the pavement, for example, rather than the line in the road. Get the child to sit or kneel or whatever in the church, at the same time showing the child his/her schedule where the time for running and shouting (preferably in a nice echoing hall) is clearly marked and the child knows what has to happen first. In some cases, especially where the child is very little, it may be best to avoid situations of temptation that are dangerous, until alternative behaviours are well accepted.

Other problems and principles for action

It is not possible in this guide to go into all the many behaviour problems that may arise in children with ASDs, but there are some principles that need to guide the way all behaviour problems are viewed and dealt with.

- Suspend your normal understanding of what the behaviour means and try to see the situation from the perspective of this particular child in this situation. What sense is s/he making of the situation? What are the likely misunderstandings? What skills or abilities are missing? What pressures or stresses are there? What would the child be saying if s/he could communicate? Get the perspective of all staff and the parents.

- Think of suitable alternatives that fulfil the same function for the child. How can these be taught? Work out a programme with all concerned.

- Does this behaviour need to be prevented or changed, or can it simply be avoided by altering the environment in some way? Wherever possible, go for the latter first, since this is by far the easier option. Also remember that it is easier for others to alter their behaviour than the child with the ASD.

- Does the behaviour need to be tackled now, or can it be left until there is a greater chance of success – the child may be more developmentally prepared? This can apply to toileting problems, where the child still has little awareness, or unreasonable expectations on young children for sitting quietly through boring events.

- Always try to emphasise a busy positive routine to replace opportunities for unwelcome behaviour with enjoyable, productive fun for all. It is the unoccupied child who is most likely to get into trouble and that applies even more so to ASDs where the children have less capacity for self-amusement.

Resources and references

Approaches

Chandler, S., Christie, P., Newson, E. & Prevezer, W. (2002) 'Developing a diagnostic and intervention package for 2 to 3 year olds with autism: outcomes of the Frameworks for Communication approach', *Autism: the International Journal of Research and Practice*, 6, 47–70.

Christie, P., Newson, E., Newson, J. & Prevezer, W. (1992) 'An interactive approach to language and communication for non-speaking children' in D. Lane & A. Miller (Eds) *Child and Adolescent Therapy*. Milton Keynes: Open University Press.

Evans, J., Castle, F. & Barraclough, S. (2001) *Making a Difference: early interventions for children with autistic spectrum disorders. LGA Research Report*. Slough: Publications Unit, NFER.

Girolametto, L.E. & Greenberg, J. (1986) 'Developing dialogue skills: the Hanen early language parent program', *Seminars in Speech and Language*, 7, 367–8.

Harris, S.L. & Handleman, J.S. (1994) *Pre-School Education Programs for Children with Autism*. Austin TX: Pro-Ed.

Hewett, D. & Nind, M. (Eds)(1998) *Interaction in Action*. London: David Fulton Publishers.

Jordan, R., Jones, G. & Murray, D. (1998) *Educational Interventions for Children with Autism: a Literature Review of Recent and Current Research*. Sudbury: DfEE Publications.

Kaufman, B. (1994) *Son-Rise: the Miracle Continues*. California: Kramer.

Keenan, M., Kerr, K.P. & Dillenburger, K. (2000) *Parents' Education as Autism Therapists: Applied Behaviour Analysis in Context*. London: Jessica Kingsley.

Kitahara, K. (1984) *Daily Life Therapy* Vols. 1, 2 & 3. Boston: Nimrod Press.

Lovaas, O.I. (1987) 'Behavioral treatment and normal intellectual and educational functioning in autistic children', *Consulting and Clinical Psychology*, 55, 3–9.

McEachin, J., Smith, T. & Lovaas, I.O. (1993) 'Long-term outcome for children with autism who received early intensive behavioral treatment', *American Journal of Mental Retardation*, 97, 359–372.

Mesibov, G. (1997) 'Formal and informal measures of the effectiveness of the TEACCH program', *Autism: the International Journal of Research and Practice*, 1, 25–35.

Murray, D.K.C. (1997) 'Autism and information technology: therapy with computers' in S. Powell & R. Jordan (Eds) *Autism and Learning: a guide to good practice*. London: David Fulton Publishers.

Nind, M. & Hewett, D. (1994) *Access to Communication*. London: David Fulton Publishers.

Peeters, T. (1997) *Autism: from Theoretical Understanding to Educational Intervention*. London: Whurr Publications.

Powell, S.D. & Jordan, R.R. (1994) 'Developing a cognitive curriculum for individuals with autism', *REACH – Journal of Special Needs Education in Ireland*, 8, 9–18.

Schopler, E. & Mesibov, G. (1995) 'Structured teaching in the TEACCH approach' in E. Schopler & G. Mesibov (Eds) *Learning and Cognition in Autism*. New York: Plenum Press.

Autistic Spectrum Disorders

Attwood, T. (1997) *Asperger's Syndrome: a Guide for Parents and Professionals*. London: Jessica Kingsley.

Cumine, V., Leach, J. & Stevenson, G. (2000) *Autism in the Early Years*. London: David Fulton Publishers.

Dawson, G. & Osterling, J. (1997) 'Early Interventions in Autism' in M. Guralnick (Ed.) *The Effectiveness of Early Intervention*. Baltimore: Brookes.

Hannah, L. (2001) *Teaching Young Children with Autistic Spectrum Disorders: a practical guide for parents and staff in mainstream schools and nurseries*. London: NAS.

Jones, G. (2002) *Educational Provision for Children with Autism and Asperger Syndrome*. London: David Fulton Publishers.

Jordan, R. (2001) *Autism with Severe Learning Difficulties: a guide for parents and professionals*. London: Souvenir Press.

Jordan, R. & Jones, G. (1999) *Meeting the Needs of Children with Autistic Spectrum Disorders*. London: David Fulton Publishers.

Jordan, R., Macleod, C. & Brunton, L. (1999) 'Making Special Schools "Specialist": a case study of the provision for pupils with autism in a school for pupils with severe learning difficulties' in G. Jones (Ed.) *GAP: Good Autism Practice*. Birmingham: University of Birmingham School of Education.

Jordan, R. & Powell, S. (1995) *Understanding and Teaching Children with Autism*. Chichester: John Wiley.

Leicestershire County Council and Fosse Health Trust (1998) *Autism: how to help your young child*. London: NAS.

Mortimer, H. (2001) *Helping Children with Autistic Spectrum Difficulties*. Leamington Spa: Scholastic.

Peeters, T. & Gillberg, C. (1999) (2nd Ed.) *Autism: Medical and Educational Aspects*. London: Whurr.

Schopler, E. & Mesibov, G. B. (Eds) (1995) *Learning and Cognition in Autism*. New York: Plenum Press.

Wing, L. (1996) *Autistic Spectrum Disorders: a guide for parents and professionals*. London: Constable.

Behaviour problems

Attwood, T. (1995) *Why Does Chris Do That?* London: NAS.

Clements, J. & Zarkowska, E. (1989) *Problem Behaviour and People with Severe Learning Difficulties: the STAR approach*. London: Chapman & Hall.

Dickinson, P. & Hannah, L. (1998) *It can get better ...: Dealing with common behaviour problems in young autistic children*. London: NAS.

Durand, M.V. (1998) *Sleep Better! A guide to improving sleep for children with special needs*. London: Paul H. Brookes.

Mortimer, H. (2000) *Developing Individual Behaviour Plans in Early Years Settings*. Tamworth: NASEN.

Wheeler, M. (1999) *Toilet Training for Individuals with Autism and Related Disorders: a comprehensive guide for parents and teachers.* London: Jessica Kingsley.

Whitaker, P. (2001) *Challenging Behaviour and Autism.* London: NAS.

Diagnosis

Howlin, P. & Moore, A. (1997) 'Diagnosis in autism: a survey of over 1,200 parents' in *Autism: the International Journal of Research and Practice*, 1, 135–162.

Jordan, R. (2001) 'Multidisciplinary work for children with autism', *Educational and Child Psychology*, 18, 2, 5–14.

Nally, B. (undated) *Diagnosis: Reactions in Families.* London: NAS.

National Autistic Society (1999) *Opening the door: a report on diagnosis and assessment of autism and Asperger syndrome based on personal experiences.* London: NAS.

Dietary treatment

Le Breton, M. (2001) *Diet Intervention and Autism: implementing the gluten free and casein free diet for autistic children and adults – a practical guide for parents.* London: Jessica Kingsley.

Shattock, P., Savery, D. & Whiteley, P. (2001) *Autism as a Metabolic Disorder: Guidelines for the implementation of a gluten and/or casein free diet.* Sunderland: Autism Research Unit.

Whiteley, P., Rodgers, J., Savery, D. & Shattock, P. (1999) 'A gluten-free diet as an intervention for autism and associated spectrum disorders: preliminary findings', *Autism: the International Journal of Research and Practice*, 3, 45–66.

Early years

Jordan, R.R. & Powell, S.D. (1990) 'High Scope – a cautionary view', *Early Years*, 11, 1, 29–34.

Mortimer, H. (2001) *The Observation and Assessment of Children in the Early Years.* Lichfield: QEd Publications.

Pre-school Learning Alliance (2002) *The Role of the Special Educational Needs Co-ordinator (SENCO) in Pre-school Settings*. London: Pre-school Learning Alliance.

Schweinhart, L.J. & Weikart, D.P. (1997) *Lasting Differences: the High/Scope Pre-school Curriculum Comparison Study through Age 23*. Ypsilanti, Michigan MN: High Scope Press.

Inclusion

Dickens, M. & Denziloe, J. (1998) *All Together: How to Create Inclusive Services for Disabled Children and their Families*. London: National Early Years Network.

Jordan, R. & Jones, G. (1996) *Educational Provision for Children with Autism in Scotland. Final report of a research project for the SOEID*. Birmingham: University of Birmingham School of Education.

Jordan, R. & Powell, S. (1994) 'Whose curriculum? Critical notes on integration and entitlement', *European Journal of Special Needs Education*, 9, 27–39.

Quill, K. (1990) 'A model for integrating children with autism', *Focus on Autistic Behaviour*, 5 (4), 1–19.

Seach, D., Lloyd, M. & Preston, M. (2002) *Supporting Children with Autism in Mainstream Schools*. Birmingham: Questions Publishing.

Official documents and guides

American Psychiatric Association (APA) (1994) *Diagnostic and Statistical Manual of Mental Disorders (DSM IV)*. Washington DC: American Psychiatric Press.

Department of Education and Science (DES: Ireland) (2001) *Educational Provision and Support for Persons with Autistic Spectrum Disorders: the Report of the Task Force on Autism*. Dublin: Irish Government Publications.

DfE (1996) *Education Act*. London: HMSO.

DfES (2001) *The SEN Toolkit*. Nottingham: DfES Publications.

DfES (2001) *Promoting Children's Mental Health within Early Years and School Settings*. Nottingham: DfES Publications.

DfES (2001) *The Special Educational Needs Code of Practice*. Nottingham: DfES Publications.

Department for Education and Skills (DfES) & Department of Health (DoH) (2002) *Autistic Spectrum Disorders: Good Practice Guidelines*. Nottingham: DfES Publications.

Department for Education and Skills (DfES) & Department of Health (DoH) (2002) *Together from the Start: Practical guidance for professionals working with disabled children (birth to 2) and their families*. Nottingham: DfES Publications.

Jordan, R., Jones, G. & Morgan, H. (2001) *Guidelines on Services for Children with Autistic Spectrum Disorders*. Mental Health Foundation/ Foundation for People with Learning Disabilities.

Medical Research Council (2001) *MRC Review of Autism Research: Epidemiology and Causes*. London: MRC.

Public Health Institute of Scotland (2001) *Autistic Spectrum Disorders: Needs Assessment Report*. Glasgow: PHIS.

Qualifications and Curriculum Authority (QCA) (2000) *Curriculum Guidance for the Foundation Stage*. Hayes: QCA Publications.

World Health Organisation (WHO) (1992) *International Classification of Diseases (ICD-10)*. Geneva: WHO.

Parents and families

Davies, J. (1995) *Children with Autism: a booklet for brothers and sisters*. Ravenshead: Early Years Centre.

Davies, J. (1995) *Children with Asperger's syndrome: a booklet for brothers and sisters*. Ravenshead: Early Years Centre.

Gilpin, R.W. (Ed.) (1993) *Laughing and Living with Autism: a collection of 'real-life' warm and humorous short stories*. New York: Future Horizons.

Gorrod, L. (1997) *My Brother Is Different*. London: NAS.

Harris, S.L. (1994) *Siblings of Children with Autism: a guide for families.* London: Woodbine House.

Ives, M. & Munro, N. (2002) *Caring for a Child with Autism.* London: Jessica Kingsley.

Jones, G., Jordan, R. & Morgan, H. (2001) *All About Autistic Spectrum Disorders: a booklet for parents and carers.* London: Mental Health Foundation.

Jordan, R. & Powell, S. (1995) 'Factors affecting school choice for parents of a child with autism', *Communication: winter,* 5–9.

National Autistic Society (2001) *The Autistic Spectrum: a parents' guide.* London: NAS.

Preece, D.R. (2000) 'An investigation into parental satisfaction with a short-term care service for children with an autistic spectrum disorder', *Good Autism Practice,* 1, 242–56.

Randall, P. & Parker, J. (1999) *Supporting the Families of Children with Autism.* Chichester: John Wiley.

Shields, J. (2001) 'NAS EarlyBird programme: partnership with parents in early intervention', *Autism: the International Journal of Research and Practice,* 5, 1, 49–56.

Sussman, F. (1999) *More than Words: a revised Hanen programme.* New Brunswick: the Hanen Centre.

Play

Beyer, J. & Gammeltoft, L. (2000) *Autism and Play.* London: Jessica Kingsley.

Jordan, R. & Libby, S. (1997) 'Developing and using play in the curriculum' in S. Powell & R. Jordan (Eds) *Autism and Learning: a guide to good practice.* London: David Fulton Publishers.

Libby, S., Powell, S., Messer, D. & Jordan, R. (1998) 'Spontaneous play in children with autism: a reappraisal', *Journal of Autism and Developmental Disorders,* 28, 487–497.

Mortimer, H. (2002) *Playladders.* Lichfield: QEd Publications.

Newman, S. (1999) *Small steps forward: using games and activities to help your pre-school child with special needs*. London: Jessica Kingsley.

Roeyers, H. (1996) 'The influence of nonhandicapped peers on the social interactions of children with pervasive developmental disorder', *Journal of Autism and Developmental Disorders* 26, 303–321.

Schuler, A.L. & Wolfberg, P.J. (2000) 'Promoting peer play and socialisation' in A.M. Wetherby & B.M. Prizant (Eds) *Autism Spectrum Disorders: A transactional developmental perspective*. London: Paul Brookes.

Sherratt, D. (1999) 'The importance of play' in G. Jones (Ed.) *Good Autism Practice: Collection of Papers 2*. School of Education, University of Birmingham.

Sherratt, D. (2002) 'Developing pretend play in children with autism: an intervention study', *Autism: the International Journal of Research and Practice*, 6, 169–180.

Sherratt, D. & Peter, M. (2002) *Developing Play and Drama in Children with Autistic Spectrum Disorders*. London: David Fulton Publishers.

Wolfberg, P. (1999) *Play and Imagination in Children with Autism*. New York: Teachers College Press.

Social and communication skills

Aldred, C. (2002) 'Child's Talk: early communication intervention for children with autism and pervasive developmental disorders', *Good Autism Practice* 3, 1, 44–57.

Barratt, P., Border, J., Joy, H., Parkinson, A., Potter, M. & Thomas, G. (2000) *Developing Pupils' Social Communication Skills: Practical resources*. London: David Fulton Publishers.

Bondy, A.S. & Frost, L.A. (1994) 'The Delaware autistic program' in S.L. Harris & J.S. Handleman (Eds) *Pre-School Educational Programs for Children with Autism*. Austin, TX: Pro-Ed.

Davies, G. (1997) 'Communication' in S. Powell & R. Jordan (Eds) *Autism and Learning: a guide to good practice*. London: David Fulton Publishers.

Potter, C. & Whittaker, C. (2000) *Enabling Communication in Children with Autism*. London: Jessica Kingsley.

Walker, M. (1980) *The Makaton Vocabulary (revised)*. Camberley: the Makaton Development Project.

Watson, L., Lord, C., Schaffer, B. & Schopler, E. (1989) *Teaching Spontaneous Communication to Autistic and Developmentally Handicapped Children*. New York: Irvington.

White, C. (2002) 'The Social Play Record: the development and evaluation of a new instrument for assessing and guiding the social interaction of children with autistic spectrum disorders', *Good Autism Practice* 3, 1, 63–78.

Special educational needs (general)

Mortimer, H. (2001) *Meeting SEN in the Early Years*. Leamington Spa: Scholastic.

Mortimer, H. (2001) *Helping Children with Learning Difficulties*. Leamington Spa: Scholastic.

Mortimer, H. (2001) *Helping Children with Physical and Co-ordination Difficulties*. Leamington Spa: Scholastic.

Mortimer, H. (2001) *Helping Children with Sensory Difficulties*. Leamington Spa: Scholastic.

Mortimer, H. (2002) *Helping Children with Speech and Language Difficulties*. Leamington Spa: Scholastic.

Mortimer, H. (2002) *Supporting Children with AD/HD and Attention Difficulties*. Lichfield: QEd Publications.

Useful organisations and journals

General addresses

Contact a Family, Equity House, 209–211 City Road, London EC1V 1JN.

DfEE Publications, PO Box 5050, Sherwood Park, Annesley, Nottingham NG15 0DG Tel: 0845 6022260; Fax: 0845 6033360; Email: dfes@prolog.uk.com; Web site: www.dfes.gov.uk/sen

Department for Education and Skills (DfES), Sanctuary Buildings, Great Smith Street, London SW1P 3BT Tel: 0870 000 2288; Fax: 01928 794248; Email: info@dfes.gov.uk; Web site: www.dfes.gov.uk

National Association for Special Educational Needs (NASEN), 4–5 Amber Business Village, Amber Close, Tamworth B77 4RP.

National Children's Bureau (NCB), 8 Wakley Street, London EC1V 1NG Tel: 020 7843 6000; Fax: 020 7278 9512; Web site: www.ncb.org.uk

National Early Years Network, 77 Holloway Road, London N7 8JZ Tel: 020 7607 9573; Fax: 020 7700 1105.

National Portage Association, 127 Monk's Dale, Yeovil, Somerset BA21 3JE Tel: 01935 71641.

Pre-school Learning Alliance, 69 Kings Cross Road, London WC1X 9LL Tel: 020 7833 0991; Fax: 020 7837 4942; Web site: www.pre-school.org.uk

Qualifications and Curriculum Authority (QCA) 83 Picadilly, London W1J 8QA Tel: 020 7509 5555; Fax: 020 7509 6666; Web site: www.qca.org.uk

Journals

Autism: the International Journal of Research and Practice Sage Publications, 6 Bonhill Street, London EC2A 4PU.

British Journal of Special Education NASEN, 4–5 Amber Business Village, Amber Close, Amington, Tamworth B77 4RP.

Focus on Autism and Other Developmental Disabilities Pro-Ed Inc., 8700 Shoal Creek Blvd., Austin, TX 78757, USA.

Good Autism Practice British Institute of Learning Disability (BILD) Campion House, Green Street, Kidderminster DY10 1JL.

Journal of Autism and Developmental Disorders Plenum Publishing, 233 Spring Street, New York, NY 10013, USA.

Special! NASEN, 4–5 Amber Business Village, Amber Close, Amington, Tamworth B77 4RP.

Special Children Questions Publishing, 27 Frederick Street, Birmingham B1 3HH.

ASD information, research and resources

Autism Cymru National Office, 6 Great Darkgate Street, Aberystwyth, Caeredigian SY23 1DE.

Autism Research Unit (diet and biochemistry), School of Pharmaceutical and Chemical Sciences, Faculty of Science, University of Sunderland, Sunderland SR2 7EE.

Centre for Social and Communication Disorders (NAS Diagnosis), Elliot House, 113 Masons Hill, Bromley, Kent BR2 9HT.

Early Years Centre, 272 Longdale Lane, Ravenshead, Notts. NG15 9AH.

National Autistic Society (NAS), 393 City Road, London EC1V 1NG.

National Portage Association, 127 Monk's dale, Yeovil, Somerset BA21 3JE.

Parents Autism Campaign for Education (PACE), 1 Floral Place, off Northampton Grove, London N1 2FS.

Autism and Computing, c/o Dinah Murray, 42 Cheverton Road, London N19 3AZ.

ASD professional bodies and training

Association of Heads and Teachers of Adults and Children with Autism (AHTACA) 1 Aston Road, Ealing, London W5 2RL.

Autism Studies (campus, distance and web-based), School of Education, University of Birmingham, Edgbaston, Birmingham B15 2TT (see *Good Autism Practice Journal* for list of other opportunities for accredited training in ASDs in the UK).

Royal College of Speech and Language Therapists, 2 White Hart Yard, London SE 1 1NX.

Web sites

ABA (Lovaas): www.lovaas.com or PEACH (Parents for Early Intervention of Autism in Children) www.peach.org.uk

Daily Life Therapy (Higashi): www.musashino-higashi.org/english.htm

Hanen: www.hanen.org/

Option (Son-Rise): www.Son-Rise.org/

PECS: www.pecs.com

TEACCH: www.unc.edu/depts/teach/